The Bhagavad Gita

VINTAGE SPIRITUAL CLASSICS

General Editors
John F. Thornton
Susan B. Varenne

ALSO AVAILABLE

The Book of Job
The Confessions of Saint Augustine
The Desert Fathers
Devotions upon Emergent Occasions
The Imitation of Christ
The Little Flowers of St. Francis of Assisi
The Rule of St. Benedict
John Henry Newman: Selected Sermons, Prayers, and Devotions

The Bhagavad Gita

TRANSLATED AND WITH

A PREFACE BY

Eknath Easwaran

VINTAGE SPIRITUAL CLASSICS

VINTAGE BOOKS
A DIVISION OF RANDOM HOUSE, INC.
NEW YORK

1850306

A VINTAGE SPIRITUAL CLASSICS ORIGINAL, APRIL 2000
FIRST EDITION

Library of Congress Cataloging-in-Publication Data
Bhagavad gita. English.
The Bhagavad gita / translated and with a preface by Eknath Easwaran.—
Abridged ed.
p.   cm.
Includes bibliographical references.
ISBN 0-375-70555-4
I. Easwaran, Eknath.   II. Title.
BL1138.62 . E5   2000
294.5'92404521—dc21   99-053439

Book design by Fritz Metsch

www.vintagebooks.com

Printed in the United States of America
10   9   8   7   6   5   4   3   2   1

CONTENTS

ABOUT THE
VINTAGE SPIRITUAL CLASSICS

by John F. Thornton and Susan B. Varenne,
General Editors

A turn or shift of sorts is becoming evident in the reflections of men and women today on their life experiences. Not quite as adamantly secular and, perhaps, a little less insistent on material satisfactions, the reading public has recently developed a certain attraction to testimonies that human life is leavened by a Presence that blesses and sanctifies. Recovery, whether from addictions or personal traumas, illness, or even painful misalignments in human affairs, is evolving from the standard therapeutic goal of enhanced self-esteem. Many now seek a deeper healing that embraces the whole person, including the soul. Contemporary books provide accounts of the invisible assistance of angels. The laying on of hands in prayer has made an appearance at the hospital bedside. Guides for the spiritually perplexed have risen to the top of best-seller lists. The darkest shadows of skepticism and unbelief, which have eclipsed the presence of the Divine in our materialistic age, are beginning to lighten and part.

If the power and presence of God are real and effective, what do they mean for human experience?

What does He offer to men and women, and what does He ask in return? How do we recognize Him? Know Him? Respond to Him? God has a reputation for being both benevolent and wrathful. Which will He be for me and when? Can these aspects of the Divine somehow be reconciled? Where is God when I suffer? Can I lose Him? Is God truthful, and are His promises to be trusted?

Are we really as precious to God as we are to ourselves and our loved ones? Do His providence and amazing grace guide our faltering steps toward Him, even in spite of ourselves? Will God abandon us if the sin is serious enough, or if we have episodes of resistance and forgetfulness? These are fundamental questions any person might address to God during a lifetime. They are pressing and difficult, often becoming wounds in the soul of the person who yearns for the power and courage of hope, especially in stressful times.

The Vintage Spiritual Classics present the testimony of writers across the centuries who have considered all these difficulties and who have pondered the mysterious ways, unfathomable mercies, and deep consolations afforded by God to those who call upon Him from out of the depths of their lives. These writers, then, are our companions, even our champions, in a common effort to discern the meaning of God in personal experience. For God is personal to us. To whom does He speak if not to us, provided we have the desire to hear Him deep within our hearts?

Each volume opens with a specially commissioned essay by a well-known contemporary writer that offers the reader an appreciation of its intrinsic value. A chronology of the general historical context of each author and his work is provided where appropriate, as are suggestions for further reading.

We offer a final word about the act of reading these spiritual classics. From the very earliest accounts of monastic practice—dating back to the fourth century—it is evident that a form of reading called *lectio divina* ("divine" or "spiritual reading") was essential to any deliberate spiritual life. This kind of reading is quite different from that of scanning a text for useful facts and bits of information, or advancing along an exciting plot line to a climax in the action. It is, rather, a meditative approach, by which the reader seeks to taste and savor the beauty and truth of every phrase and passage. This process of contemplative reading has the effect of enkindling in the reader compunction for past behavior that has been less than beautiful and true. At the same time, it increases the desire to seek a realm where all that is lovely and unspoiled may be found. There are four steps in *lectio divina*: first, to read, next to meditate, then to rest in the sense of God's nearness, and, ultimately, to resolve to govern one's actions in the light of new understanding. This kind of reading is itself an act of prayer. And, indeed, it is in prayer that God manifests His Presence to us.

by Eknath Easwaran

Many years ago, when I was still a graduate student, I traveled by train from central India to Simla, then the summer seat of the British government in India. We had not been long out of Delhi when suddenly a chattering of voices disturbed my reverie. I asked the man next to me if something had happened. "Kurukshetra!" he replied. "The next stop is Kuruk-shetra!"

I could understand the excitement. Kurukshetra, "the field of the Kurus," is the setting for the climactic battle of the *Mahabharata,* the vastest epic in any world literature, on which virtually every Hindu child in India is raised. Its characters, removed in time by some three thousand years, are as familiar to us as our relatives. The temper of the story is utterly contemporary; I can imagine it unfolding in the nuclear age as easily as in the dawn of Indian history. The *Mahabharata* is literature at its greatest— in fact, it has been called a literature in itself, comparable in its breadth and depth and characterization to the whole of Greek literature or Shakespeare. But what makes it unique is that embedded in this literary masterpiece is one of the finest mystical documents the world has seen: the Bhagavad Gita.

I must have heard the Gita recited hundreds of times when I was growing up, but I don't suppose it had any special significance for me then. Not until I went to college and met Mahatma Gandhi did I begin to understand why nothing in the long, rich stretch of Indian culture has had a wider appeal, not only within India but outside as well. Today, after more than fifty years of devoted study, I would not hesitate to call it India's most important gift to the world. The Gita has been translated into every major language and perhaps a hundred times into English alone; commentaries on it are said to be more numerous than on any other scripture. Like the Sermon on the Mount, it has an immediacy that sweeps away time, place, and circumstance. Addressed to everyone, of whatever background or status, the Gita distills the loftiest truths of India's ancient wisdom into simple, memorable poetry that haunts the mind and informs the affairs of everyday life.

Everyone in our car got down from the train to wander for a few minutes on the now peaceful field. Thousands of years ago this was Armageddon. The air rang with conch horns and the shouts of battle for eighteen days. Great phalanxes shaped like eagles and fish and the crescent moon surged back and forth in search of victory, until in the end almost every warrior in the land lay slain.

"Imagine!" my companion said to me in awe. "Bhishma and Drona commanded their armies here.

Arjuna rode here, with Sri Krishna himself as his charioteer. Where you're standing now—who knows?—Arjuna might have sat, his bow and arrows on the ground, while Krishna gave him the words of the Bhagavad Gita."

The thought was thrilling. I felt the way Schliemann must have when he finally reached that desolate bluff in western Turkey and knew he was standing "on the ringing plains of windy Troy," walking the same ground as Achilles, Odysseus, Hector, and Helen. Yet at the same time, I felt I knew the setting of the Gita much more intimately than I could ever know this peaceful field. The battlefield is a perfect backdrop, but the Gita's subject is the war within, the struggle for self-mastery that every human being must wage if he or she is to emerge from life victorious.

The Gita and Its Setting

Historians surmise that, like the *Iliad,* the *Mahabharata* might well be based on actual events, culminating in a war that took place somewhere between 1000 and 700 B.C.E.—close, that is, to the dawn of recorded Indian history. This guess has recently been supported by excavations at the ancient city of Dvaraka, which, according to the *Mahabharata,* was destroyed and submerged in the sea after the departure of its divine ruler, Krishna. Only five hundred years or so before this, by generally accepted guess, Aryan tribes originally from the Caucasus had invaded the Indian subcontinent and imposed their martial civilization on the peoples they found, bringing the prototype of the Sanskrit language and countless elements of belief and culture that have been part of the Hindu tradition ever since. The oldest part of the most ancient of Hindu scriptures, the Rig Veda, dates from this period—about 1500 B.C.E., if not earlier.

Yet the real sources of Indian religious faith, I believe, must be traced to a much earlier epoch. When the Aryans entered the Indian subcontinent through the mountains of the Hindu Kush, they encountered a civilization on the banks of the Indus River that archaeologists date back as far as 3000 B.C.E. Roughly contemporaneous with the pyramid builders on the Nile, these Indus dwellers achieved a comparable level of technology. They had metalworkers skilled in sheet making, riveting, and casting of copper and bronze, crafts and industries with standardized methods of production, land and sea trade with cultures as far away as Mesopotamia, and well-planned cities with water supply and public sanitation systems unequaled until the Romans. Evidence suggests that they may have used a decimal system of measurement. But, most remarkable, it is apparently here and not with the Aryans that the great spiritual discoveries of Hinduism originated. Images of Shiva as Yogeshvara, the Lord of Yoga, suggest that meditation was practiced in a civilization that flourished a millennium before the Vedas were committed to an oral tradition.

If this is so, it would imply that the same systematic attitude the Indus Valley dwellers applied to their technology was applied to the study of the mind. This was *Brahmavidya,* the "supreme science"—supreme because whereas other sciences studied the external world, Brahmavidya sought knowledge of an underlying reality that would inform all other studies and activities.

Whatever its origins, in the early part of the first millennium B.C.E. we find clearly stated both the methods and the discoveries of Brahmavidya. With this introspective tool the inspired *rishis* (literally "seers") of ancient India analyzed their awareness of human experience to see if there was anything in it that was absolute. Their findings can be summarized in three statements that Aldous Huxley, following Leibniz, has called the Perennial Philosophy because they appear in every age and civilization: (1) there is an infinite, changeless reality beneath the world of change; (2) this same reality lies at the core of every human personality; (3) the purpose of life is to discover this reality experientially: that is, to realize God while here on earth. These principles and the interior experiments for realizing them were taught systematically in "forest academies" or ashrams—a tradition that continues unbroken after some three thousand years.

The discoveries of Brahmavidya were systematically committed to memory (and eventually to writing) in the Upanishads, visionary documents that are the earliest and purest statement of the Perennial Philosophy. How many of these precious records once existed no one knows; some 108 have survived as part of the Hindu canon of authority, the four

Vedas. All have one unmistakable hallmark: the vivid stamp of personal mystical experience. These are records of direct encounter with the divine. Tradition calls them *shruti:* literally "heard," as opposed to learned; they are their own authority.

By convention, only the Vedas (including their Upanishads) are considered shruti, based on direct knowledge of God. All other Indian scriptures—including, by this criterion, the Bhagavad Gita—are secondary, dependent on the higher authority of the Vedas. However, this is a conventional distinction and one that might disguise the nature of the documents it classifies. In the literal sense the Gita too is shruti, owing its authority not to other scriptures but to the fact that it set down the direct mystical experience of a single author, Shankara, a towering mystic of the ninth century C.E. whose word carries the authority of Augustine, Eckhart, and Aquinas all in one, must have felt this, for in selecting the minimum sources of Hinduism, he passed over almost a hundred Upanishads of Vedic authority to choose ten central Upanishads and the Bhagavad Gita.

The Gita, I would argue, is not an integral part of the *Mahabharata.* It is essentially an Upanishad, and my conjecture is that it was set down by an inspired seer (traditionally Vyasa) and inserted into the epic at the appropriate place. Other fragments seem to have been added in this way to the *Mahabharata* and to other popular secondary scriptures; it is an effective method of preserving new material in an oral tradition. There is also traditional weight behind this idea, for as far back as anyone can trace, each chapter of the Gita has ended with the same formula: "In the Bhagavad-Gita Upanishad, the text on the supreme science [*Brahmavidya*] of yoga, this is the chapter entitled . . ."

Finally, by way of further support, we can observe that, except for its first chapter, which sets the stage, the Gita not only does not develop the action of the *Mahabharata* but rather is at odds with it. Battle lines are drawn—the climax of decades of dissension—and on the eve of combat Prince Arjuna loses his nerve and asks his charioteer, Krishna, what to do. Then what? Krishna—no ordinary charioteer but an incarnation of God—enters into some seven hundred verses of sublime instruction on the nature of the soul and its relation to God, the levels of consciousness and reality, the makeup of the phenomenal world, and so on, culminating in a stupendous mystical experience in which he reveals himself to Arjuna as the transcendent Lord of life and death. He counsels Arjuna to be compassionate to friend and enemy alike, to see himself in every person, to suffer others' sorrows as his own. Then the Gita is over, the narration picks up again, and battle is joined—a terrible, desperate slaughter compromising everyone's honor, by the end of which Arjuna's side emerges victorious. Only great genius would have placed the Gita in such a dramatic setting, but it stands out from the rest as a timeless, practical manual for daily living.

To those who take this dramatic setting as part of the spiritual instruction and get entangled in the question of the Gita justifying war, Mahatma Gandhi had a practical answer: simply base your life on the Gita sincerely and systematically and see if you find killing or even hurting others compatible with its teachings. (He made the same point concerning the Sermon on the Mount.) The very heart of the Gita's message is to see the Lord in every creature and act accordingly, and the scripture is full of verses to spell out what this means:

> I am ever present to those who have realized me in every creature. Seeing all life as my manifestation, they are never separated from me. They worship me in the hearts of all, and all their actions proceed from me. Wherever they live, they abide in me. (6:30–31)

> When a person responds to the joys and sorrows of others as if they were his own, he has attained the highest state of spiritual union. (6:32)

> That one I love who is incapable of ill will, who is friendly and compassionate . . . who looks upon friend and foe with equal regard. (12:13, 18)

> He alone sees truly who sees the Lord the same in every creature, who sees the Deathless in the hearts of all that die. Seeing the same Lord everywhere, he does not harm himself or others. Thus he attains the supreme goal. (13:27–28)

Scholars can debate the point forever, but when the Gita is practiced, I think, it becomes clear that the struggle it is concerned with is the struggle for self-mastery. It was Vyasa's genius to take the whole great *Mahabharata* epic and see it as metaphor for the perennial war between the forces of light and the forces of darkness in every human heart. Arjuna and Krishna are then no longer merely characters in a literary masterpiece. Arjuna becomes Everyman, asking the Lord himself, Sri Krishna, the perennial questions about life and death—not as a philosopher but as the quintessential man of action. Thus read, the Gita is not an external dialogue but an internal one: between the ordinary human personality, full of questions about the meaning of life, and our deepest Self, which is divine.

There is, in fact, no other way to read the Gita and grasp it as spiritual instruction. If I could offer only one key to understanding this divine dialogue, it would be to remember that it takes place in the depths of consciousness and that Krishna is not some external being, human or superhuman, but the spark of divinity that lies at the core of the human personality. This is not literary or philosophical conjecture; Krishna says as much to Arjuna over and over. "I am the true Self in the heart of every creature, Arjuna, and the beginning, middle, and end of their existence" (10:20).

In such statements the Gita distills the essence of the Upanishads, not piecemeal but comprehensively, offering their lofty insights as a manual not of philosophy but of everyday human activity—a handbook of the Perennial Philosophy unique in world history.

The Upanishadic Background

The Gita, naturally enough, takes for granted that its audience is familiar with the basic ideas of Hindu religious thought, almost all of which can be found in the Upanishads. It also uses some technical vocabulary from yoga psychology. All this needs to be explained in contemporary terms if the modern reader is to grasp what is essential and timeless in the Gita's message and not get bogged down in strange terminology.

First, however, the non-Hindu faces a third obstacle: the multiplicity of names used for aspects of God. From the earliest times, Hinduism has proclaimed one God while accommodating worship of him (or her, for to millions God is the Divine Mother) in many different names. "Truth is one," says a famous verse of the Rig Veda; "people call it by various names." A monastic devotee might find that Shiva embodies the austere detachment he seeks; a devotee who wants to live "in the world," partaking of its innocent pleasures but devoted to service of her fellow creatures, might find in Krishna the perfect incarnation of her ideals. In every case, this clothing of the Infinite in human form serves to focus a devotee's love and to provide an inspiring ideal. But whatever form is worshiped, it is only an aspect of the same one God.

In the Gita—in fact, virtually everywhere in Hindu myth and scripture—we also encounter "the gods" in the plural. These are the *devas,* deities that seem to have come in with the Aryans and that have recognizable counterparts in other Aryan-influenced cultures: Indra, god of war and storm; Varuna, god of waters and a moral overseer; Agni, god of fire, the Hermes-like intermediary between heaven and earth; and so on. The Gita refers to the devas as being worshiped by those who want to propitiate natural and supernatural powers, in much the same way ancestors were worshiped. In modern terms, they can best be understood as personifying the forces of nature.

This question out of the way, we can proceed to the Upanishadic background the Gita assumes.

Atman and Brahman

The Upanishads are not systematic philosophy; they are more like ecstatic slide shows of mystical experience—vivid, disjointed, stamped with the power of direct, personal encounter with the divine. If they seem to embrace contradictions, that is because they do not try to smooth over the seams of these experiences. They simply set down what the rishis saw, viewing the ultimate reality from different levels of spiritual awareness, like snapshots of the same object from different angles: now seeing God as utterly transcendent, for example, now seeing God as immanent as well. These differences are not of practical importance, and the Upanishads agree on their central ideas: *Brahman,* the Godhead; *Atman,* the divine core of personality; *dharma,* the law that expresses and maintains the unity of creation; *karma,* the web of cause and effect; *samsara,* the cycle of birth and death; and *moksha,* the spiritual liberation that is life's supreme goal.

Even while ancient India was making breakthroughs in the natural sciences and mathematics, the sages of the Upanishads were turning inward to analyze the data that nature presents to the mind. Beneath the senses they found not a world of solid, separate objects but a ceaseless process of change—matter coming together, dissolving, and coming together again in a different form. Below this flux of things with "name and form," however, they found something changeless: an infinite, indivisible reality in which the transient data of the world cohere. They called this reality Brahman: the Godhead, the divine ground of existence.

In examining our knowledge of ourselves, the sages made a similar discovery. Instead of a single coherent personality, they found layer upon layer of components—senses, emotions, will, intellect, ego—each in flux. At different times and in different company, the same person seems to have different personalities. Moods shift and flicker; desires and opinions change with time. Change is the nature of the mind. The sages observed this flow of thoughts and sensations and asked, "Then where am I?" The parts do not add up to a whole; they just flow by.

Like physical phenomena, the mind is a field of forces, no more the seat of intelligence than radiation or gravity is. Just as the world dissolves into a sea of energy, the mind dissolves into a river of impressions and thoughts, a flow of fragmentary data that do not hold together.

Western philosophers reasoned their way to a similar conclusion, but with them it was intellectual exercise. These ancient sages were actually exploring the mind. In profound meditation, they found that when consciousness is so acutely focused that it is utterly withdrawn from the body and mind it enters a kind of singularity in which the sense of a separate ego disappears. In this state, the supreme climax of meditation, the seers discovered a core of consciousness beyond time and change. They called it simply Atman, the Self.

I have described the discovery of Atman and Brahman—God immanent and God transcendent—as separate, but there is no real distinction. In the climax of meditation, the sages discovered *unity:* the same indivisible reality without and within. It was *advaita,* "not two." The Chandogya Upanishad says epigrammatically, *Tat tvam asi:* "Thou art That." Atman is Brahman: the Self in each person is not different from the Godhead.

Nor is it different from person to person. The Self is one, the same in every creature. This is not some peculiar tenet of the Hindu scriptures; it is the testimony of everyone who has undergone these experiments in the depths of consciousness and followed them through to the end. Here is Ruysbroeck, a great mystic of medieval Europe; every word is carefully chosen:

> The image of God is found essentially and personally in all mankind. Each possesses it entire and undivided, and all together not more than one alone. In this way we are all one, intimately united in our eternal image, which is the image of God and the source in us of all our life.

In the unitive experience, every trace of separateness disappears; life is a seamless whole. But the body cannot remain in this state for long. After a while, awareness of mind and body returns, and then the conventional world of multiplicity rushes in again with such vigor and vividness that the memory of unity, though stamped with reality, seems as distant as a dream. The unitive state has to be entered over and over until we are established in it. But once established, even in the midst of ordinary life, we see the One underlying the many, the Eternal beneath the ephemeral.

The disciplines for achieving this are called *yoga,* as is the state of union: the word comes from the root *yuj,* to yoke or bind together. The "experience" itself (properly speaking, it is beyond experience) is called *samadhi.* And the state attained is called *moksha* or *nirvana,* both of which signify going beyond the conditioning of time, space, and causality.

In this state the individual realizes that he is not a

physical creature but the Atman, the Self, and thus not separate from God. He sees the world not as pieces but whole, and he sees that whole as a manifestation of God. Once identified with the Self, he knows that, although his body will die, he will not die; his awareness of this identity is not ruptured by the death of the physical body. Thus he has realized the essential immortality that is the birthright of every human being. To such a person, the Gita says, death is no more traumatic than taking off an old coat (2:13, 22).

Life cannot offer any higher realization. The supreme goal of human existence has been attained. The man or woman who realizes God has everything and lacks nothing (6:22). Life cannot threaten such a person; all it holds is the opportunity to love, to serve, and to give.

Dharma, Karma, Rebirth, and Liberation

It has been said that if you understand just two words, *dharma* and *karma,* you will have grasped the essence of Hinduism. This is a simplification, but it would be difficult to exaggerate the importance of these concepts. Both are deeply embedded in Hindu thought, and the Gita, like other Hindu scriptures, takes them for granted, not as theoretical premises but as facts of life that can be verified in personal experience.

The word *dharma* means many things, but its underlying sense is "that which supports," from the root *dhri,* "to support, hold up, or bear." Generally, *dharma* implies support from within: the essence of a thing, its virtue, that which makes it what it is.

An old story illumines this meaning with the highest ideal of Hinduism. A sage, seated beside the Ganges, notices a scorpion that has fallen into the water. He reaches down and rescues it, only to be stung. Some time later he looks down and sees the scorpion thrashing about in the water again. Once more he reaches down to rescue it, and once more he is stung. A bystander, observing all this, exclaims, "Holy One, why do you keep doing that? Don't you see that the wretched creature will only sting you in return?" "Of course," the sage replied. "It is the dharma of a scorpion to sting. But it is the dharma of a human being to save."

On a larger scale, *dharma* means the essential order of things, an integrity and harmony in the universe and the affairs of life that cannot be disturbed without courting chaos. Thus it means rightness, justice, goodness, purpose rather than chance. An ancient Sanskrit epigram states, *Ahimsa paramo dharma:* the highest dharma is *ahimsa,* nonviolence, universal love for all living creatures; for every kind of violence is a violation of dharma, the fundamental law of the unity of life.

Underlying this idea is the oneness of life: the Upanishadic discovery that all things are interconnected because at its deepest level creation is indivisible. This oneness bestows a basic balance on the whole of nature such that any disturbance in one place has to send ripples everywhere, as a perfect bubble, touched lightly in one place, trembles all over until balance is restored. The implications are caught perfectly by those famous lines from Donne, which deserve to be read now with a fresh eye as not merely great rhetoric but a faithful representation of reality:

No man is an island, entire of itself; every man is a piece of the continent, a part of the main; if a clod be washed away by the sea, Europe is the less, as well as if a promontory were, as well as if a manor of thy friend's or of thine own were; any man's death diminishes me, because I am involved in mankind; and therefore never send to know for whom the bell tolls, it tolls for thee.

Thus every act or thought has consequences, which themselves will have consequences; life is the most intricate web of interconnections. This is the law of karma, one of the most important and least understood ideas in ancient Indian thought. The word *karma* is repeated so often in the Gita that I want to illustrate it in some detail: some intuitive sense of karma as an organic law makes Krishna's teachings a good deal clearer.

Literally, *karma* means "something that is done." Often it can be translated as "deed" or "action." The law of karma states simply that every event is both a cause and an effect. Every act has consequences of a similar kind, which in turn have further consequences and so on; and every act, every karma, is also the consequence of some previous karma.

This refers not only to physical action but to mental activity as well. In their analysis of the phenomenal world and the world within, the sages of the Upanishads found that there is not merely an accidental but an essential relationship between mental and physical activity. Given appropriate conditions to develop further, thoughts breed actions of the same kind, as a seed can grow only into one particular kind of tree.

Plainly put, the law of karma says that whatever you do will come back to you. If Joe hits Bob, and later Ralph hits Joe, that is Joe's karma coming back to him. This sounds occult because we do not see all the connections. But the connections are there, and the law of karma is no more occult than the law of gravitation. It states that that blow has to have consequences; it cannot end with Bob getting a black eye. It makes an impression on Bob's consciousness—predictably, he gets furious—and it makes an impression on Joe's consciousness as well.

Let us trace it first through Bob. He might take revenge on Joe then and there, simply by hitting him back: I call this cash karma, where you do something and pay for it immediately. In these times, however, it is more likely that Bob will suppress his feelings, so that the consequences of Joe's blow will not show up until later—probably in ways that seem to have nothing to do with Joe or his fist.

Karma is rarely as simple as this illustration, but in any case it should be clear that Bob's anger at Joe will have repercussions throughout his relationships. Those repercussions will have repercussions—

say Bob goes home and explodes at his wife, and his wife gets angry at Ralph's wife, who takes it out on Ralph, who works with Joe; and the next time Joe irritates Ralph, Ralph lets him have it. Poor Joe, rubbing his chin, can't have the slightest idea that he is being repaid for hitting Bob. All he feels is anger at Ralph: and so the chain of consequences continues, and Joe's karmic comeuppance becomes the seed of a new harvest.

Most people have no idea how many others are affected by their behavior and example. This perception gives some idea of how complex the web of karma actually is. No one, of course, has the omniscience to see this picture fully. But the idea of a network of such connections, far from being occult, is natural and plausible. The law of karma states unequivocally that, though we cannot see the connections, we can be sure everything that happens to us, good and bad, originated once in something we did or thought. It follows that we can change what happens to us by changing ourselves; we can take our destiny into our own hands.

Karma is sometimes considered punitive, a matter of getting one's just deserts. But it is much more illuminating to consider karma an educative force whose purpose is to teach the individual to act in harmony with dharma—not to pursue selfish interests at the expense of others but to contribute to life and consider the welfare of the whole. In this sense life is like a school: one can learn, one can graduate, one can skip a grade or stay behind. As long as a debt of karma remains, however, a person has to keep coming back for further education. That is the basis of *samsara*, the cycle of birth and death.

A good many misleading words have been written on this last point, largely because of the fascination that reincarnation seems to hold in the West. Rightly understood, however, reincarnation is not exotic but quite natural. If personality consists of several sheaths, the body being only the outermost, there is no reason why personality should die when the body is shed. The sages of the Upanishads saw personality as a field of forces. Packets of karma to them were forces that have to work themselves out; if the process is interrupted by death, those forces remain until conditions allow them to work again in a new context.

Sleep can illustrate the dynamics of this idea. When we sleep we pass in and out of two stages, dreaming and dreamless sleep. In the first, consciousness is withdrawn from the body and senses but still engaged in the mind. In dreamless sleep, however, consciousness is withdrawn from the mind as well. Then the thinking process—even the sense of "I"—is temporarily suspended, and consciousness is said to rest in the Self. In this state a person ceases to be a separate creature, a separate personality. In dreamless sleep, the Upanishads say, a king is not a king nor a pauper poor; no one is old or young, male or female, educated or ignorant. When consciousness returns to the mind, however, the thinking process starts up again, and personality returns to the body.

According to this analysis, the ego dies every night. Every morning we pick up our desires where we left off—the same people, yet a little different, too. The Upanishads describe dying as a very similar process. Consciousness is withdrawn from the body into the senses, from the senses into the mind, and then consolidated in the ego; when the body is finally wrenched away, the ego remains, a potent package of desires and karma. And as a person's last waking thoughts shape his dreams, the contents of the unconscious at the time of death—the residue of all he has thought and desired and lived for in the past—determine the context of his next life. He takes a body again, the sages say, to come back to just the conditions where his desires and karma can be fulfilled. Those who have realized the Self, however, have no karma to work out, no personal desires. At the time of death they are absorbed into the Lord:

> But they for whom I am the supreme goal, who do all work renouncing self for me and meditate on me with single-hearted devotion, these I will swiftly rescue from the fragment's cycle of birth and death, for their consciousness has entered into me. (12:6–7)

Yoga Psychology

In trying to describe their discoveries, the Upanishadic seers developed a specialized vocabulary. The most useful part of this vocabulary comes from a philosophical system called Sankhya, which has much in common with the Buddhist philosophy that followed it. Its practical counterpart is the school of meditation called Yoga. An ancient saying celebrates their universality: "There is no theory like Sankhya, no practice like Yoga."

The Gita does not actually belong to the Sankhya school or to any other; it is as comprehensive as the Upanishads. But no philosophy provides a more precise vocabulary than Sankhya for describing the workings of the mind, and the Gita draws on that vocabulary freely.

Sankhya philosophy posits two separate categories: *Purusha,* spirit, and *prakriti,* everything else. This is not the Western mind-matter distinction. *Prakriti* is the field of what can be known objectively, the field of phenomena, the world of whatever has "name and form"; that is, not only of matter and energy but also of the mind. As physics postulates a unified field from which all phenomena can be derived, Sankhya describes a field that includes mental phenomena as well. Thus mind, energy, and matter lie on a continuum—a field of forces. Purusha, pure spirit, is the knower of this field of phenomena and belongs to a wholly different order of reality. Only Purusha is conscious—or, rather, Purusha is consciousness itself. What we call "mind" is only an internal instrument that Purusha uses, just as the body is its external instrument. For practical purposes—at least as far as the Gita is concerned—*Purusha* may be regarded as a synonym for *Atman.* Purusha is the Self, beyond all change, the same in every creature.

Sankhya describes prakriti as made up of forces called *gunas,* three basic states of energy: *tamas,* inertia; *rajas,* activity; and *sattva,* harmony or equilibrium. Every state of matter and mind is a combination of these three. They can be illustrated by comparison with the three states of matter in classical physics: solid, liquid, and gas. Tamas is frozen energy, the resistance of inertia. A block of ice has a good deal of energy in the chemical bonds that hold it together, but the energy is locked in, bound up, rigid. When the ice melts, some of that energy is released as the water flows; similarly, rajas—activity—is like a swollen river, full of uncontrolled power. And sattva, harmony, can be compared to steam when its power is harnessed. These are very imprecise parallels, but they convey an important point about the gunas: all three are states of energy, and each can be converted into the others.

According to Sankhya, everything in the world of mind and matter is an expression of all three gunas, with one guna always predominant. This becomes particularly interesting in describing personality as a field of forces. The rajasic person is full of energy, the tamasic person is sluggish, indifferent, insensitive; the sattvic person is calm, resourceful, compassionate, and selfless. Yet all three states are always present in each of us at some level of awareness, and their proportions change: their interplay is the dynamics of personality. The same individual will have times when he is bursting with energy and times when inertia descends and paralyzes his will, times when she is thoughtful and other times when she is moving so fast that she never notices those around her. The person is the same; he or she is simply experiencing the play of the gunas.

As long as we identify with our body and mind, we are at the mercy of this play. But the Self is not involved in the gunas' interaction. It is witness rather than participant:

> Without senses itself, it shines through the functioning of the senses. Completely independent, it supports all things. Beyond the gunas, it enjoys their play. (13:14)

Because personality is a process, the human personality is constantly remaking itself. Left on its own, the mind goes on repeating the same old habitual patterns. But by training the mind, the Gita says, anyone can learn to step in and change old ways of thinking. That is the central principle of yoga:

> Reshape yourself through the power of your will; never let yourself be degraded by self-will. The will is the only friend of the Self, and the will is the only enemy of the Self. (6:5)

This is the dynamic of spiritual evolution. In its natural state, consciousness is a continuous flow of awareness. But through the distorting action of the gunas, we have fallen from this native state into separate, self-centered awareness. Looking through a divided mind, we see life divided everywhere: separate people, antagonistic interests, conflicts within ourselves. Evolution, according to the Gita, is a painfully slow return to our native state. First tamas must be transformed into rajas—apathy and insensitiveness into energetic, enthusiastic activity. But the energy of rajas is self-centered and dispersed; it must be harnessed to a higher ideal by the will. Then it becomes sattva, when all this passionate energy is channeled into selfless action. This state is marked by happiness, a calm mind, abundant vitality, and the concentration of genius.

But even this is not the end. The goal of evolution is to return to unity; that is, to still the mind. Then the soul rests in pure, unitary consciousness, which is a state of permanent joy:

> In the still mind, in the depths of meditation, the Self reveals itself. Beholding the Self by means of the Self, an aspirant knows the joy and peace of complete fulfillment. (6:20)

The Essence of the Gita

The Gita does not present a system of philosophy. It offers something to every seeker after God, of whatever temperament, by whatever path. The reason for this universal appeal is that it is basically practical: it is a handbook for Self-realization and a guide to action.

Some scholars will find practicality a tall claim, because the Gita is full of lofty and even abstruse philosophy. Yet even its philosophy is not there to satisfy intellectual curiosity; it is meant to explain to a spiritual aspirant why he is asked to undergo certain disciplines. Like any handbook, the Gita makes most sense when it is practiced.

As the traditional chapter titles put it, the Gita is *Brahmavidyayam yogashastra,* a textbook on the supreme science of yoga. But *yoga* is a word with many meanings—as many, perhaps, as there are paths to Self-realization. What kind of yoga does the Gita teach?

The common answer is that it presents three yogas or even four—the four main paths of Hindu mysticism. In *jnana yoga,* the yoga of knowledge, an aspirant uses his will and discrimination to disidentify himself from his body, mind, and senses until he knows he is nothing but the Self. The follower of *bhakti yoga,* the yoga of devotion, achieves the same goal by identifying himself completely with the Lord in love; by and large, this is the path taken by most of the mystics of Christianity, Judaism, and Islam. In *karma yoga,* the yoga of selfless action, the aspirant dissolves his identification with body and mind by identifying with the whole of life, forgetting his finite self in the service of others. And the follower of *raja yoga,* the yoga of meditation, disciplines his mind and senses until the mind-process is suspended in a healing stillness and he merges in the Self.

Thus the Gita offers something for every kind of spiritual aspirant, and for two thousand years each of the major schools of Indian philosophy has quoted the Gita in defense of its particular claims. This fluidity sometimes exasperates scholars, who feel the Gita contradicts itself. It also puzzled Arjuna, the faithful representative of you and me. "O Krishna," he says at the beginning of Chapter 3, "you have said that knowledge [*jnana*] is greater than action [*karma*]; why then do you ask me to wage this terrible war? Your advice seems inconsistent. Give me one path to follow to the supreme good" (3:1–2). No doubt he speaks for every reader at this point, and for those who go on wanting one path only, the confusion simply grows worse.

For those who try to practice the Gita, however, there is a thread of inner consistency running through Krishna's advice. Like a person walking around the same object, the Gita takes more than one point of view. Whenever Krishna describes one of the traditional paths to God, he looks at it from the inside, extolling its virtues over the others. For the time being, that is the path; when he talks about yoga, he means that particular yoga. Thus "this ancient word" *yoga,* said Gandhi's intimate friend and secretary, Mahadev Desai,

> is pressed by the Gita into service to mean the entire gamut of human endeavor to storm the gates of heaven. [It means] the yoking of all the powers of the body and the mind and soul to God; it means the discipline of the intellect, the mind, the emotions, the will, which such a yoking presupposes; it means a poise of the soul which enables one to look at life in all its aspects and evenly.

The Gita brings together all the specialized senses of the word *yoga* to emphasize their common meaning: the sum of what one must do to realize God.

The thread through Krishna's teaching, the essence of the Gita, can be given in one word: renunciation. This is the common factor in the four yogas. It is a bleak word in English, conjuring up the austerity and self-deprivation enjoined in the monastic orders—the "poverty, chastity, and obedience" so perfectly embodied by Francis of Assisi. When the Gita promises "freedom through renunciation," the impression most of us get is that we are being asked to give up everything we want out of life; in this drab state, having lost whatever we value, we will be free from sorrow. Who wants that kind of freedom?

But this is not at all what the Gita means. It does not even enjoin material renunciation, although it certainly encourages simplicity. As always, its emphasis is on the mind. It teaches that we can become free by giving up not material things but selfish attachments to material things—and, more important, to people. It asks us to renounce not the enjoyment of life but the clinging to selfish enjoyment at whatever cost to others. It pleads, in a word, for the renunciation of selfishness in thought, word, and action—a theme that is common to all mystics, Western and Eastern alike. Work hard in the world without any selfish attachment, the Gita counsels, and you will purify your consciousness of self-will. In this way any man or woman can gradually attain freedom from the bondage of selfish conditioning.

This is a mental discipline, not just a physical one,

and I want to repeat that, to understand the Gita, it is important to look beneath the surface of its injunctions and see the mental state involved. Philanthropic activity can benefit others and still carry a large measure of ego involvement. Such work is good, but it is not yoga. It may benefit others, but it will not necessarily benefit the doer. Everything depends on the state of mind. Action without selfish motive purifies the mind; the doer is less likely to be ego-driven later. The same action done with a selfish motive entangles a person further, precisely by strengthening that motive so it is more likely to prompt selfish action again.

In the Gita this is said in many ways, and from differences in language it may seem that Krishna is giving different pieces of advice. In practice, however, it becomes evident that these are only various ways of saying the same thing.

To begin with, Krishna often tells Arjuna to "renounce the fruits of action":

> You have the right to work, but never to the fruit of work. You should never engage in action for the sake of reward, nor should you long for inaction. Perform work in this world, Arjuna, as a man established within himself—without selfish attachments, and alike in success and defeat. For yoga is perfect evenness of mind. (2:47–48)

"Fruits," of course, means the outcomes. What Krishna means is to give up attachment to the results of what you do: that is, to give your best to every undertaking without insisting that the results work out the way you want, or even whether what you do is pleasant or unpleasant. Mahatma Gandhi explained with the authority of his personal experience:

> By detachment I mean that you must not worry whether the desired result follows from your action or not, so long as your motive is pure, your means correct. Really, it means that things will come right in the end if you take care of the means and leave the rest to Him.

"But renunciation of fruit," Gandhi warned,

> in no way means indifference to the result. In regard to every action one must know the result that is expected to follow, the means thereto, and the capacity for it. He who, being thus equipped, is without desire for the result and is yet wholly engrossed in the due fulfillment of the task before him, is said to have renounced the fruits of his action.

This attitude frees a person completely. Whatever comes—success or failure, praise or blame, victory or defeat—he can give his best with a clear, unruffled mind. Nothing can shake his courage or break his will; no setback can depress her or make her feel burned out. As the Gita says, "Yoga is skill in action" (2:50).

Again, Krishna repeatedly tells Arjuna to surrender everything to him in love. But this is not different advice, merely different words. Krishna is asking Arjuna to act entirely for his sake, not for any personal gain. The whole point of the path of love is to transform motivation from "I, I, I," to "thou, thou, thou"—that is, to surrender selfish attachments by dissolving them in the desire to give.

Meister Eckhart said eloquently of this state:

> Whoever has God in mind, simply and solely God, in all things, such a man carries God with him into all his works and into all places, and God alone does all his works. He seeks nothing but God; nothing seems good to him but God. He becomes one with God in every thought. Just as no multiplicity can dissipate God, so nothing can dissipate this man or make him multiple.

Thus we arrive at the idea of "actionless action": of individuals so established in identification with the Self that in the midst of tireless service to those around them, they remain in inner peace, the still witness of action. They do not act, the Gita says; it is the Self that acts through them: "They alone see truly who see that all actions are performed by prakriti, while the Self remains unmoved" (13:29).

Again, this is a universal testimony. Here is one of the most active of mystics, St. Catherine of Genoa:

> When the soul is naughted and transformed, then of herself she neither works nor speaks nor wills, nor feels nor hears nor understands; neither has she

of herself the feeling of outward or inward, where she may move. And in all things it is God who rules and guides her, without the mediation of any creature. And the state of this soul is then a feeling of such utter peace and tranquility that it seems to her that her heart, and her bodily being, and all both within and without, is immersed in an ocean of utmost peace. . . . And she is so full of peace that though she press her flesh, her nerves, her bones, no other thing comes forth from them than peace.

Again, when the Gita talks about "inaction in the midst of action" (4:18, et cetera), we can call on Ruysbroeck to illuminate the seeming paradox. The person who has realized God, he said, mirrors both his aspects: "tranquility according to His essence, activity according to His nature: absolute repose, absolute fecundity." And he added,

The interior person lives his life according to these two ways; that is to say, in rest and in work. And in each of them he is wholly and undividedly; for he dwells wholly in God in virtue of his restful fruition and wholly in himself in virtue of his active love. . . . This is the supreme summit of the inner life.

This is the only kind of inaction the Gita recommends. It is not possible to do nothing, Krishna says; the very nature of the mind is to be active. The Gita's goal is to harness this activity in selfless service, removing the poisonous agency of the ego:

"As long as one has a body, one cannot renounce action altogether. True renunciation is giving up all desire for personal reward" (18:11). Eckhart explained,

> Either one must learn to have God in his work and hold fast to him there, or he must give up his work altogether. Since, however, man cannot live without activities that are both human and various, we must learn to keep God in everything we do, and whatever the job or place, keep on with him, letting nothing stand in our way.

It would be difficult to find a better summary of the Gita's message anywhere—and this, incidentally, from a man considered to represent the path of knowledge.

A Higher Image

Perhaps the clearest way to grasp the Gita is to look at how it describes those who embody its teachings. There are portraits like this at the beginning of the Gita, the middle, and the end, each offering a model of our full human potential.

The first is given at the end of Chapter 2 (2:54–72), verses that Gandhi said hold the key to the entire Gita. Arjuna has just been told about Self-knowledge; now he asks a very practical question: When a person attains this knowledge, how does it show? How do such people conduct themselves in everyday life? We expect a list of virtues. Instead,

Krishna delivers a surprise: the surest sign is that they have banished all selfish desires. Their senses and mind are completely trained, so they are free from sensory cravings and self-will. Identified completely with the Self, not with body or mind, they realize their immortality here on earth.

The implications of this reply are not spelled out; we have to see them in a living person. G. K. Chesterton once said that to understand the Sermon on the Mount we should look not at Jesus but at St. Francis. To understand the Gita I went to look at Mahatma Gandhi, who had done his best for forty years to translate those verses into his daily life. Seeing him, I understood that those "who see themselves in all and all in them" would simply not be capable of harming others. (Augustine said daringly, "Love, then do as you like": nothing will then come out of you but goodness.) I saw too what it meant to view one's body with detachment: not indifference but compassionate care as an instrument of service. I saw what it means to rest in the midst of intense action. Most important, I grasped one of the most refreshing ideas in Hindu mysticism: original goodness. Since the Self is the core of every personality, no one needs to acquire goodness and compassion; they are already there. All that is necessary is to remove the selfish habits that hide them.

Chapter 12 gives another portrait in its closing verses (12:13–20), and here we do get an inspiring list of the marks of those who follow the path of love:

That one I love who is incapable of ill will, who is friendly and compassionate. Living beyond the reach of *I* and *mine* and of pleasure and pain, patient, contented, self-controlled, firm in faith, with all his heart and all his mind given to me—with such a one I am in love. (12:13–14)

Finally comes the passionate description with which the Gita ends, when Krishna tells Arjuna how to recognize the man or woman who has reached life's supreme goal:

He who is free from selfish attachments, who has mastered himself and his passions, attains the supreme perfection of freedom from action. Listen and I shall explain now, Arjuna, how one who has attained perfection also attains Brahman, the supreme consummation of wisdom. (18:49 20)

These are not separate paths, separate ideals. All three passages describe one person: vital, active, compassionate, self-reliant in the highest sense, for he or she looks to the Self for everything and needs nothing from life but the opportunity to give. In brief, such a person knows who he is, and in that knowing is everything.

This is not running away from life, as is so often claimed. It is running into life, open-handed, open-armed: "flying, running, and rejoicing," said Thomas à Kempis, for "he is free and will not be bound"—will never be entangled in self-doubt, conflict, or vacillation. Far from being desireless—look at Gandhi, Catherine of Siena, St. Teresa, St. Francis—the man or woman who realizes God has yoked all human passions to the overriding desire to give and love and serve; in that unification we can see not the extinction of personality but its full blossoming. This is what it means to be fully human; our ordinary lives of stimulus and response, getting and spending, seem by comparison as faint as remembered dreams. One of the most appealing features of the Gita for our times is that it clears up misunderstandings about the spiritual life and shows it for what it is: active, joyful, intentional, a middle path between extremes that transfigures everyday living.

Spiritual Evolution

One last untranslatable concept and I will let the Gita speak for itself. That concept is *shraddha,* and its nearest English equivalent is *faith.* I have translated it as such, but *shraddha* means much more. It is literally "that which is placed in the heart": all the beliefs we hold so deeply that we never think to question them. It is the set of values, axioms, prejudices, and prepossessions that colors our perceptions, governs our thinking, dictates our responses, and shapes our lives, generally without our even being aware of its presence and power.

This may sound philosophical, but shraddha is not an intellectual abstraction. It is our very substance. The Gita says, "A person is what his shraddha is" (17:3). The Bible uses almost the same words: "As a man thinketh in his heart, so is he." Shraddha reflects everything that we have made ourselves and points to what we have become.

But there is nothing passive about shraddha. It is full of potency, for it prompts action, conditions behavior, and determines how we see and therefore respond to the world around us. When St. John of the Cross said, "We live in what we love," he was explaining shraddha. Our lives are an eloquent expression of our belief: what we deem worth having, doing, attaining, being. What we strive for shows what we value; we back our shraddha with our time, our energy, our very lives.

Thus shraddha determines destiny. As the Buddha put it, "All that we are is the result of what we have thought. We are made of our thoughts; we are molded by our thoughts." As we think, so we become. This is true not only of individuals but of societies, institutions, and civilizations, according to the dominant ideas that shape their actions. To take just one example, faith in technology is part of the shraddha of modern civilization.

"Right shraddha," according to the Gita, is faith in spiritual laws: in the unity of life, the presence of divinity in every person, the essentially spiritual nature of the human being. "Wrong shraddha" is not necessarily morally wrong, merely ignorant. It means believing that there is no more to life than physical existence, that the human being is only a biochemical entity, that happiness can be got by pursuing private interests and ignoring the rest of life. Such beliefs are misplaced: we have attached our shraddha to beliefs that life cannot bear out. Sooner or later they must prove false, and then our shraddha changes.

Like our thinking, therefore—like us ourselves—shraddha evolves. The purpose of karma is to teach the consequences of shraddha, so that by trial and error, life after life, the individual soul acquires the kind of faith that leads to fulfillment of life's supreme goal.

This is perhaps the most compassionate insight into human evolution ever expressed. The Gita is steeped in it, but it is not exclusive to the Gita or to Hinduism. "Whether you like it or not, whether you know it or not," said Meister Eckhart, "secretly Nature seeks and hunts and tries to ferret out the track in which God may be found." The whole purpose of every experience, every activity, every faculty, is to turn the human being inward and lead us back to our divine source. Thus every person seeking satisfaction in the world outside—pleasure, power, profit, prestige—is really looking for God: "As men approach me, so I receive them. All paths, Arjuna, lead to me" (4:11).

Two forces pervade human life, the Gita says: the upward thrust of evolution and the downward pull of our evolutionary past. Ultimately, then, the Gita is not a book of commandments but a book of choices. It does mention sin, but mostly it talks about ignorance and its consequences. Krishna tells Arjuna about the Self, the forces of the mind, the relationship between thought and action, the law of karma, and then concludes, "I give you these precious words of wisdom; reflect on them and then do as you choose" (18:63). The struggle is between two halves of human nature, and choices are posed every moment.

Everyone who has accepted this challenge, I think, will testify that life offers no fiercer battle than this war within. We have no choice about the fighting; it is built into human nature. But we do have the choice of which side to fight on:

> Remembering me, you shall overcome all difficulties through my grace. But if you will not heed me in your self-will, nothing will avail you. If you egotistically say, "I will not fight this battle," your resolve will be useless; your own nature will drive you into it. (18:58–59) Therefore, remember me at all times and fight on. With your heart and mind intent on me, you will surely come to me. (8:7)

Thus the Gita places human destiny entirely in human hands. Its world is not deterministic, but neither is it an expression of blind chance: we shape ourselves and our world by what we believe and think and act on, whether for good or for ill. In this sense the Gita opens not on Kurukshetra but on dharmakshetra, the field of dharma, where Arjuna and Krishna are standing for us all.

The Bhagavad Gita

Chapter 1
THE WAR WITHIN

DHRITARASHTRA:

1 O Sanjaya, tell me what happened at Kuruk-
shetra, the field of dharma, where my family
and the Pandavas gathered to fight.

SANJAYA:

2 Having surveyed the forces of the Pandavas
arrayed for battle, prince Duryodhana
approached his teacher, Drona, and spoke.

3 "O my teacher, look at this mighty army of
the Pandavas, assembled by your own gifted dis-

4 ciple, Yudhishthira. There are heroic warriors
and great archers who are the equals of Bhima
and Arjuna: Yuyudhana, Virata, the mighty

5 Drupada, Dhrishtaketu, Chekitana, the
valiant king of Kashi, Purujit, Kuntibhoja,

6 the great leader Shaibya, the powerful Yudha-
manyu, the valiant Uttamaujas, and the son of
Subhadra, in addition to the sons of Draupadi.
All these command mighty chariots.

7 "O best of brahmins, listen to the names of
those who are distinguished among our own

8 forces: Bhishma, Karna, and the victorious
Kripa; Ashvatthama, Vikarna, and the son

9 of Somadatta. There are many others, too,

[3]

heroes giving up their lives for my sake, all
proficient in war and armed with a variety of
10 weapons. Our army is unlimited and com-
manded by Bhishma; theirs is small and com-
11 manded by Bhima. Let everyone take his
proper place and stand firm supporting
Bhishma!"

12 Then the powerful Bhishma, the grandsire,
oldest of all the Kurus, in order to cheer
Duryodhana, roared like a lion and blew his
13 conch horn. And after Bhishma, a tremen-
dous noise arose of conchs and cowhorns
and pounding on drums.

14 Then Sri Krishna and Arjuna, who were
standing in a mighty chariot yoked with
15 white horses, blew their divine conchs. Sri
Krishna blew the conch named Panchajanya,
and Arjuna blew that called Devadatta. The
mighty Bhima blew the huge conch Paundra.
16 Yudhishthira, the king, the son of Kunti,
blew the conch Anantavijaya; Nakula and
17 Sahadeva blew their conchs as well. Then the
king of Kashi, the leading bowman, the great
warrior Shikhandi, Dhrishtadyumna, Virata,
18 the invincible Satyaki, Drupada, all the sons
of Draupadi, and the strong-armed son of
19 Subhadra joined in, and the noise tore
through the heart of Duryodhana's army.
Indeed, the sound was tumultuous, echoing
throughout heaven and earth.

20 Then, O Dhritarashtra, lord of the earth,
having seen your son's forces set in their
places and the fighting about to begin, Arjuna
spoke these words to Sri Krishna:

ARJUNA:

21 O Krishna, drive my chariot between the
22 two armies. I want to see those who desire to
fight with me. With whom will this battle be
23 fought? I want to see those assembled to fight
for Duryodhana, those who seek to please the
evil-minded son of Dhritarashtra by engaging
in war.

SANJAYA:

24 Thus Arjuna spoke, and Sri Krishna, driving
his splendid chariot between the two armies,
25 facing Bhishma and Drona and all the kings of
the earth, said: "Arjuna, behold all the Kurus
gathered together."

26 And Arjuna, standing between the two
armies, saw fathers and grandfathers,
teachers, uncles, and brothers, sons and
27 grandsons, in-laws and friends. Seeing his
kinsmen established in opposition, Arjuna
was overcome by sorrow. Despairing, he
spoke these words:

ARJUNA:

28 O Krishna, I see my own relations here anx-
29 ious to fight, and my limbs grow weak; my
mouth is dry, my body shakes, and my hair is
30 standing on end. My skin burns, and the bow
Gandiva has slipped from my hand. I am un-
able to stand; my mind seems to be whirling.
31 These signs bode evil for us. I do not see that
any good can come from killing our relations
32 in battle. O Krishna, I have no desire for vic-
tory, or for a kingdom or pleasures. Of what
33 use is a kingdom or pleasure or even life, if
those for whose sake we desire these things—
34 teachers, fathers, sons, grandfathers, uncles,
in-laws, grandsons, and others with family
ties—are engaging in this battle, renouncing
35 their wealth and their lives? Even if they were
to kill me, I would not want to kill them, not
even to become ruler of the three worlds.
How much less for the earth alone?

36 O Krishna, what satisfaction could we find
in killing Dhritarashtra's sons? We would
become sinners by slaying these men, even
37 though they are evil. The sons of Dhritarash-
tra are related to us; therefore, we should not
kill them. How can we gain happiness by kill-
ing members of our own family?

38 Though they are overpowered by greed and
see no evil in destroying families or injuring

39 friends, *we* see these evils. Why shouldn't we
40 turn away from this sin? When a family de-
clines, ancient traditions are destroyed. With
them are lost the spiritual foundations for life,
41 and the family loses its sense of unity. Where
there is no sense of unity, the women of the
family become corrupt; and with the corrup-
tion of its women, society is plunged into
42 chaos. Social chaos is hell for the family and
for those who have destroyed the family as
well. It disrupts the process of spiritual evolu-
43 tion begun by our ancestors. The timeless
spiritual foundations of family and society
would be destroyed by these terrible deeds,
which violate the unity of life.

44 It is said that those whose family dharma has
45 been destroyed dwell in hell. This is a great
sin! We are prepared to kill our own relations
out of greed for the pleasures of a kingdom.
46 Better for me if the sons of Dhritarashtra,
weapons in hand, were to attack me in battle
and kill me unarmed and unresisting.

SANJAYA:

47 Overwhelmed by sorrow, Arjuna spoke these
words. And casting away his bow and his
arrows, he sat down in his chariot in the mid-
dle of the battlefield.

Chapter 2
THE ILLUMINED MAN

1 These are the words that Sri Krishna spoke to
the despairing Arjuna, whose eyes were burn-
ing with tears of pity and confusion.

SRI KRISHNA:

2 This despair and weakness in a time of crisis
are mean and unworthy of you, Arjuna. How
have you fallen into a state so far from the

3 path to liberation? It does not become you to
yield to this weakness. Arise with a brave
heart and destroy the enemy.

ARJUNA:

4 How can I ever bring myself to fight against
Bhishma and Drona, who are worthy of rev-

5 erence? How can I, Krishna? Surely it would
be better to spend my life begging than to kill
these great and worthy souls! If I killed them,
every pleasure I found would be tainted. I

6 don't even know which would be better, for
us to conquer them or for them to conquer us.
The sons of Dhritarashtra have confronted us;
but why would we care to live if we killed
them?

7 My will is paralyzed, and I am utterly con-
   fused. Tell me which is the better path for me.
   Let me be your disciple. I have fallen at your
8 feet; give me instruction. What can overcome
   a sorrow that saps all my vitality? Even power
   over men and gods or the wealth of an empire
   seems empty.

SANJAYA:

9 This is how Arjuna, the great warrior, spoke
   to Sri Krishna. With the words, "O Krishna, I
   will not fight," he fell silent.
10 As they stood between the two armies, Sri
   Krishna smiled and replied to Arjuna, who
   had sunk into despair.

SRI KRISHNA:

11 You speak sincerely, but your sorrow has no
   cause. The wise grieve neither for the living
12 nor for the dead. There has never been a time
   when you and I and the kings gathered here
   have not existed, nor will there be a time
13 when we will cease to exist. As the same
   person inhabits the body through childhood,
   youth, and old age, so too at the time of death
   he attains another body. The wise are not
   deluded by these changes.

14 When the senses contact sense objects, a
   person experiences cold or heat, pleasure or
   pain. These experiences are fleeting; they
   come and go. Bear them patiently, Arjuna.

15 Those who are not affected by these changes,
who are the same in pleasure and pain, are
truly wise and fit for immortality. Assert your
strength and realize this!

16 The impermanent has no reality; reality
lies in the eternal. Those who have seen the
boundary between these two have attained the

17 end of all knowledge. Realize that which per-
vades the universe and is indestructible; no
power can affect this unchanging, imperish-

18 able reality. The body is mortal, but he who
dwells in the body is immortal and immeasur-
able. Therefore, Arjuna, fight in this battle.

19 One man believes he is the slayer, another
believes he is the slain. Both are ignorant;

20 there is neither slayer nor slain. You were
never born; you will never die. You have
never changed; you can never change.
Unborn, eternal, immutable, immemorial,

21 you do not die when the body dies. Realizing
that which is indestructible, eternal, unborn,
and unchanging, how can you slay or cause
another to slay?

22 As a man abandons worn-out clothes
and acquires new ones, so when the body is
worn out a new one is acquired by the Self,
who lives within.

23 The Self cannot be pierced by weapons or
burned by fire; water cannot wet it, nor can

24 the wind dry it. The Self cannot be pierced or
burned, made wet or dry. It is everlasting and
infinite, standing on the motionless founda-

25 tions of eternity. The Self is unmanifested,
beyond all thought, beyond all change.
Knowing this, you should not grieve.

26 O mighty Arjuna, even if you believe the Self
to be subject to birth and death, you should

27 not grieve. Death is inevitable for the living;
birth is inevitable for the dead. Since these are

28 unavoidable, you should not sorrow. Every
creature is unmanifested at first and then
attains manifestation. When its end has come,
it once again becomes unmanifested. What is
there to lament in this?

29 The glory of the Self is beheld by a few, and
a few describe it; a few listen, but many with-

30 out understanding. The Self of all beings,
living within the body, is eternal and cannot
be harmed. Therefore, do not grieve.

31 Considering your dharma, you should not
vacillate. For a warrior, nothing is higher than

32 a war against evil. The warrior confronted
with such a war should be pleased, Arjuna,

33 for it comes as an open gate to heaven. But if
you do not participate in this battle against
evil, you will incur sin, violating your dharma
and your honor.

34 The story of your dishonor will be repeated
endlessly: and for a man of honor, dishonor is
35 worse than death. These brave warriors will
think you have withdrawn from battle out of
fear, and those who formerly esteemed you
36 will treat you with disrespect. Your enemies
will ridicule your strength and say things that
should not be said. What could be more pain-
ful than this?

37 Death means the attainment of heaven; victory
means the enjoyment of the earth. Therefore
38 rise up, Arjuna, resolved to fight! Having
made yourself alike in pain and pleasure,
profit and loss, victory and defeat, engage in
this great battle and you will be freed from
sin.

39 You have heard the intellectual explanation of
Sankhya, Arjuna; now listen to the principles
of yoga. By practicing these you can break
40 through the bonds of karma. On this path
effort never goes to waste, and there is no
failure. Even a little effort toward spiritual
awareness will protect you from the greatest
fear.

41 Those who follow this path, resolving deep
within themselves to seek me alone, attain
singleness of purpose. For those who lack
resolution, the decisions of life are many-
branched and endless.

42 There are ignorant people who speak flowery
words and take delight in the letter of the law,

43 saying that there is nothing else. Their hearts
are full of selfish desires, Arjuna. Their idea of
heaven is their own enjoyment, and the aim of
all their activities is pleasure and power. The
fruit of their actions is continual rebirth.

44 Those whose minds are swept away by the
pursuit of pleasure and power are incapable of
following the supreme goal and will not attain
samadhi.

45 The scriptures describe the three gunas. But
you should be free from the action of the
gunas, established in eternal truth, self-
controlled, without any sense of duality or
the desire to acquire and hoard.

46 Just as a reservoir is of little use when the
whole countryside is flooded, scriptures are of
little use to the illumined man or woman,
who sees the Lord everywhere.

47 You have the right to work, but never to
the fruit of work. You should never engage
in action for the sake of reward, nor should

48 you long for inaction. Perform work in this
world, Arjuna, as a man established within
himself—without selfish attachments, and
alike in success and defeat. For yoga is perfect
evenness of mind.

49 Seek refuge in the attitude of detachment and
you will amass the wealth of spiritual aware-
ness. Those who are motivated only by desire
for the fruits of action are miserable, for they
are constantly anxious about the results of
50 what they do. When consciousness is unified,
however, all vain anxiety is left behind. There
is no cause for worry, whether things go well
or ill. Therefore, devote yourself to the disci-
plines of yoga, for yoga is skill in action.

51 The wise unify their consciousness and aban-
don attachment to the fruits of action, which
binds a person to continual rebirth. Thus they
attain a state beyond all evil.

52 When your mind has overcome the confusion
of duality, you will attain the state of holy in-
difference to things you hear and things you
53 have heard. When you are unmoved by the con-
fusion of ideas and your mind is completely
united in deep samadhi, you will attain the state
of perfect yoga.

ARJUNA:

54 Tell me of those who life established in wis-
dom, ever aware of the Self, O Krishna. How
do they talk? How sit? How move about?

SRI KRISHNA:

55 They live in wisdom who see themselves in
all and all in them, who have renounced every

[14]

selfish desire and sense craving tormenting the
heart.

56 Neither agitated by grief nor hankering after
pleasure, they live free from lust and fear
and anger. Established in meditation, they are
57 truly wise. Fettered no more by selfish attach-
ments, they are neither elated by good fortune
nor depressed by bad. Such are the seers.

58 Even as a tortoise draws in its limbs, the wise
59 can draw in their senses at will. Aspirants ab-
stain from sense pleasures, but they still crave
for them. These cravings all disappear when
60 they see the highest goal. Even of those who
tread the path, the stormy senses can sweep
61 off the mind. They live in wisdom who subdue
their senses and keep their minds ever absorbed
in me.

62 When you keep thinking about sense objects,
attachment comes. Attachment breeds desire,
63 the lust of possession that burns to anger. An-
ger clouds the judgment; you can no longer
learn from past mistakes. Lost is the power to
choose between what is wise and what is un-
64 wise, and your life is utter waste. But when
you move amidst the world of sense, free
65 from attachment and aversion alike, there
comes the peace in which all sorrows end,
and you live in the wisdom of the Self.

66 The disunited mind is far from wise; how
    can it meditate? How be at peace? When you
    know no peace, how can you know joy?

67 When you let your mind follow the call of the
    senses, they carry away your better judgment
    as storms drive a boat off its charted course on
    the sea.

68 Use all your power to free the senses from
    attachment and aversion alike, and live in the

69 full wisdom of the Self. Such a sage awakes to
    light in the night of all creatures. That which
    the world calls day is the night of ignorance to
    the wise.

70 As rivers flow into the ocean but cannot make
    the vast ocean overflow, so flow the streams
    of the sense-world into the sea of peace that is
    the sage. But this is not so with the desirer of
    desires.

71 They are forever free who renounce all selfish
    desires and break away from the ego-cage of
    "I," "me," and "mine" to be united with the

72 Lord. This is the supreme state. Attain to this,
    and pass from death to immortality.

Chapter 3
SELFLESS SERVICE

ARJUNA:

1 O Krishna, you have said that knowledge is
   greater than action; why then do you ask me
2 to wage this terrible war? Your advice seems
   inconsistent. Give me one path to follow to
   the supreme good.

SRI KRISHNA:

3 At the beginning of time I declared two paths
   for the pure heart: *jnana yoga,* the contempla-
   tive path of spiritual wisdom, and *karma yoga,*
   the active path of selfless service.

4 He who shirks action does not attain free-
   dom; no one can gain perfection by abstain-
5 ing from work. Indeed, there is no one who
   rests for even an instant; every creature is
   driven to action by his own nature.

6 Those who abstain from action while allow-
   ing the mind to dwell on sensual pleasure can-
7 not be called sincere spiritual aspirants. But
   they excel who control their senses through
   the mind, using them for selfless service.

8 Fulfill all your duties; action is better than
inaction. Even to maintain your body,
9 Arjuna, you are obliged to act. Selfish action
imprisons the world. Act selflessly, without
any thought of personal profit.

10 At the beginning, mankind and the obligation
of selfless service were created together.
"Through selfless service, you will always
be fruitful and find the fulfillment of your
desires": this is the promise of the Creator.

11 Honor and cherish the devas as they honor
and cherish you; through this honor and love
12 you will attain the supreme good. All human
desires are fulfilled by the devas, who are
pleased by selfless service. But anyone who
enjoys the things given by the devas without
offering selfless acts in return is a thief.

13 The spiritually minded, who eat in the spirit
of service, are freed from all their sins; but the
selfish, who prepare food for their own satis-
14 faction, eat sin. Living creatures are nourished
by food, and food is nourished by rain; rain
itself is the water of life, which comes from
selfless worship and service.

15 Every selfless act, Arjuna, is born from
Brahman, the eternal, infinite Godhead. He is
16 present in every act of service. All life turns
on this law, O Arjuna. Whoever violates it,

indulging his senses for his own pleasure and
ignoring the needs of others, has wasted his
17 life. But those who realize the Self are always
satisfied. Having found the source of joy and
fulfillment, they no longer seek happiness
18 from the external world. They have nothing
to gain or lose by any action; neither people
nor things can affect their security.

19 Strive constantly to serve the welfare of
the world; by devotion to selfless work one
20 attains the supreme goal of life. Do your
work with the welfare of others always in
mind. It was by such work that Janaka
attained perfection; others, too, have
followed this path.

21 What the outstanding person does, others
will try to do. The standards such people
create will be followed by the whole world.
22 There is nothing in the three worlds for me to
gain, Arjuna, nor is there anything I do not
have; I continue to act, but I am not driven
23 by any need of my own. If I ever refrained
from continuous work, everyone would im-
24 mediately follow my example. If I stopped
working I would be the cause of cosmic
chaos, and finally of the destruction of this
world and these people.

25 The ignorant work for their own profit,
Arjuna; the wise work for the welfare of the

26 world, without thought for themselves. By abstaining from work you will confuse the ignorant, who are engrossed in their actions. Perform all work carefully, guided by compassion.

27 All actions are performed by the gunas of prakriti. Deluded by his identification with

28 the ego, a person thinks, "*I* am the doer." But the illumined man or woman understands the domain of the gunas and is not attached. Such people know that the gunas interact with each other; they do not claim to be the doer.

29 Those who are deluded by the operation of the gunas become attached to the results of their action. Those who understand these

30 truths should not unsettle the ignorant. Performing all actions for my sake, completely absorbed in the Self, and without expectations, fight!—but stay free from the fever of the ego.

31 Those who live in accordance with these divine laws without complaining, firmly established in faith, are released from karma.

32 Those who violate these laws, criticizing and complaining, are utterly deluded, and are the cause of their own suffering.

33 Even a wise man acts within the limitations of his own nature. Every creature is subject to

34 prakriti; what is the use of repression? The senses have been conditioned by attraction to the pleasant and aversion to the unpleasant. Do not be ruled by them; they are obstacles in your path.

35 It is better to strive in one's own dharma than to succeed in the dharma of another. Nothing is ever lost in following one's own dharma, but competition in another's dharma breeds fear and insecurity.

ARJUNA:

36 What is the force that binds us to selfish deeds, O Krishna? What power moves us, even against our will, as if forcing us?

SRI KRISHNA:

37 It is selfish desire and anger, arising from the guna of rajas; these are the appetites and evils which threaten a person in this life.

38 Just as a fire is covered by smoke and a mirror is obscured by dust, just as the embryo rests deep within the womb, knowledge is hidden
39 by selfish desire—hidden, Arjuna, by this unquenchable fire for self-satisfaction, the inveterate enemy of the wise.

40 Selfish desire is found in the senses, mind, and intellect, misleading them and burying
41 the understanding in delusion. Fight with

all your strength, Arjuna! Controlling your senses, conquer your enemy, the destroyer of knowledge and realization.

42 The senses are higher than the body, the mind higher than the senses; above the mind is the intellect, and above the intellect
43 is the Atman. Thus, knowing that which is supreme, let the Atman rule the ego. Use your mighty arms to slay the fierce enemy that is selfish desire.

Chapter 4
WISDOM IN ACTION

SRI KRISHNA:

1 I told this eternal secret to Vivasvat.
Vivasvat taught Manu, and Manu taught
2 Ikshvaku. Thus, Arjuna, eminent sages
received knowledge of yoga in a continuous
tradition. But through time the practice of
yoga was lost in the world.

3 The secret of these teachings is profound. I
have explained them to you today because
you are my friend and devotee.

ARJUNA:

4 You were born much after Vivasvat; he lived
very long ago. Why do you say that you
taught this yoga in the beginning?

SRI KRISHNA:

5 You and I have passed through many births,
Arjuna. You have forgotten, but I remember
them all.

6 My true being is unborn and changeless.
I am the Lord who dwells in every creature.
Through the power of my own maya, I
manifest myself in a finite form.

7   Whenever dharma declines and the purpose of life is forgotten, I manifest myself on earth.

8   I am born in every age to protect the good, to destroy evil, and to reestablish dharma.

9   He who knows me as his own divine Self breaks through the belief that he is the body and is not reborn as a separate creature. Such a

10   one, Arjuna, is united with me. Delivered from selfish attachment, fear, and anger, filled with me, surrendering themselves to me, purified in the fire of my being, many have reached the state of unity in me.

11   As men approach me, so I receive them.

12   All paths, Arjuna, lead to me. Those desiring success in their actions worship the gods; through action in the world of mortals, their desires are quickly fulfilled.

13   The distinctions of caste, guna, and karma have come from me. I am their cause, but I myself am changeless and beyond all action.

14   Actions do not cling to me because I am not attached to their results. Those who understand this and practice it live in freedom.

15   Knowing this truth, aspirants desiring liberation in ancient times engaged in action. You too can do the same, pursuing an active life in the manner of those ancient sages.

16 What is action and what is inaction? This
question has confused the greatest sages. I
will give you the secret of action, with which
17 you can free yourself from bondage. The true
nature of action is difficult to grasp. You
must understand what is action and what is
inaction, and what kind of action should be
avoided.

18 The wise see that there is action in the midst
of inaction and inaction in the midst of action.
Their consciousness is unified, and every act is
done with complete awareness.

19 The awakened sages call a person wise when
all his undertakings are free from anxiety
about results; all his selfish desires have been
20 consumed in the fire of knowledge. The wise,
ever satisfied, have abandoned all external
supports. Their security is unaffected by the
results of their action; even while acting, they
21 really do nothing at all. Free from expecta-
tions and from all sense of possession, with
mind and body firmly controlled by the Self,
they do not incur sin by the performance of
physical action.

22 They live in freedom who have gone beyond
the dualities of life. Competing with no one,
they are alike in success and failure and con-
23 tent with whatever comes to them. They are
free, without selfish attachments; their minds

are fixed in knowledge. They perform all
work in the spirit of service, and their karma
is dissolved.

24 The process of offering is Brahman; that
which is offered is Brahman. Brahman offers
the sacrifice in the fire of Brahman. Brahman
is attained by those who see Brahman in every
action.

25 Some aspirants offer material sacrifices to the
gods. Others offer selfless service as sacrifice
26 in the fire of Brahman. Some renounce all en-
joyment of the senses, sacrificing them in the
fire of sense restraint. Others partake of sense
objects but offer them in service through the
27 fire of the senses. Some offer the workings
of the senses and the vital forces through the
fire of self-control, kindled in the path of
knowledge.

28 Some offer wealth; others offer sense restraint
and suffering. Some take vows and offer
knowledge and study of the scriptures; and
29 some make the offering of meditation. Some
offer the forces of vitality, regulating their in-
halation and exhalation, and thus gain control
30 over these forces. Others offer the forces of
vitality through restraint of their senses. All
these understand the meaning of service and
will be cleansed of their impurities.

31 True sustenance is in service, and through it a
man or woman reaches the eternal Brahman.
But those who do not seek to serve are with-
out a home in this world. Arjuna, how can
they be at home in any world to come?

32 These offerings are born of work, and each
guides mankind along a path to Brahman.
Understanding this, you will attain liberation.

33 The offering of wisdom is better than any
material offering, Arjuna; for the goal of all
work is spiritual wisdom.

34 Approach someone who has realized the pur-
pose of life and question him with reverence
and devotion; he will instruct you in this wis-

35 dom. Once you attain it, you will never again
be deluded. You will see all creatures in the
Self, and all in me.

36 Even if you were the most sinful of sinners,
Arjuna, you could cross beyond all sin by the

37 raft of spiritual wisdom. As the heat of a fire
reduces wood to ashes, the fire of knowledge

38 burns to ashes all karma. Nothing in this
world purifies like spiritual wisdom. It is the
perfection achieved in time through the path
of yoga, the path which leads to the Self
within.

39 Those who take wisdom as their highest
goal, whose faith is deep and whose senses

are trained, attain wisdom quickly and enter
40 into perfect peace. But the ignorant, indecisive and lacking in faith, waste their lives. They can never be happy in this world or any other.

41 Those established in the Self have renounced selfish attachments to their actions and cut through doubts with spiritual wisdom. They
42 act in freedom. Arjuna, cut through this doubt in your own heart with the sword of spiritual wisdom. Arise; take up the path of yoga!

Chapter 5

RENOUNCE AND REJOICE

ARJUNA:

1 O Krishna, you have recommended both the path of selfless action and *sannyasa,* the path of renunciation of action. Tell me definitely which is better.

SRI KRISHNA:

2 Both renunciation of action and the selfless performance of action lead to the supreme goal. But the path of action is better than renunciation.

3 Those who have attained perfect renunciation are free from any sense of duality; they are unaffected by likes and dislikes, Arjuna, and are free from the bondage of self-will. The im-
4 mature think that knowledge and action are different, but the wise see them as the same. The person who is established in one path
5 will attain the rewards of both. The goal of knowledge and the goal of service are the same; those who fail to see this are blind.

6 Perfect renunciation is difficult to attain without performing action. But the wise, follow-

ing the path of selfless service, quickly reach
Brahman.

7 Those who follow the path of service, who
have completely purified themselves and con-
quered their senses and self-will, see the Self
in all creatures and are untouched by any
action they perform.

8 Those who know this truth, whose con-
sciousness is unified, think always, "I am not
the doer." While seeing or hearing, touching
or smelling; eating, moving about, or sleep-
9 ing; breathing or speaking, letting go or hold-
ing on, even opening or closing the eyes, they
understand that these are only the movements
of the senses among sense objects.

10 Those who surrender to Brahman all selfish
attachments are like the leaf of a lotus floating
clean and dry in water. Sin cannot touch
11 them. Renouncing their selfish attachments,
those who follow the path of service work
with body, senses, and mind for the sake of
self-purification.

12 Those whose consciousness is unified aban-
don all attachment to the results of action and
attain supreme peace. But those whose desires
are fragmented, who are selfishly attached to
the results of their work, are bound in every-
thing they do.

13 Those who renounce attachment in all their
deeds live content in the "city of nine gates,"
the body, as its master. They are not driven to
act, nor do they involve others in action.

14 Neither the sense of acting, nor actions, nor
the connection of cause and effect comes from
the Lord of this world. These three arise from
nature.

15 The Lord does not partake in the good and
evil deeds of any person; judgment is clouded
16 when wisdom is obscured by ignorance. But
ignorance is destroyed by knowledge of the
Self within. The light of this knowledge
shines like the sun, revealing the supreme
17 Brahman. Those who cast off sin through this
knowledge, absorbed in the Lord and estab-
lished in him as their one goal and refuge, are
not reborn as separate creatures.

18 Those who possess this wisdom have equal
regard for all. They see the same Self in a spir-
itual aspirant and an outcaste, in an elephant, a
19 cow, and a dog. Such people have mastered
life. With even mind they rest in Brahman,
who is perfect and is everywhere the same.
20 They are not elated by good fortune nor
depressed by bad. With mind established in
21 Brahman, they are free from delusion. Not
dependent on any external support, they real-
ize the joy of spiritual awareness. With con-

sciousness unified through meditation, they
live in abiding joy.

22 Pleasures conceived in the world of the senses
have a beginning and an end and give birth to
misery, Arjuna. The wise do not look for
23 happiness in them. But those who overcome
the impulses of lust and anger which arise in
the body are made whole and live in joy.
24 They find their joy, their rest, and their light
completely within themselves. United with
the Lord, they attain nirvana in Brahman.

25 Healed of their sins and conflicts, working
for the good of all beings, the holy sages
26 attain nirvana in Brahman. Free from anger
and selfish desire, unified in mind, those who
follow the path of yoga and realize the Self are
established forever in that supreme state.

27 Closing their eyes, steadying their breathing,
and focusing their attention on the center of
28 spiritual consciousness, the wise master their
senses, mind, and intellect through medita-
tion. Self-realization is their only goal. Freed
from selfish desire, fear, and anger, they live
29 in freedom always. Knowing me as the friend
of all creatures, the Lord of the universe, the
end of all offerings and all spiritual disciplines,
they attain eternal peace.

Chapter 6

THE PRACTICE OF MEDITATION

SRI KRISHNA:

1 It is not those who lack energy or refrain from action, but those who work without expectation of reward who attain the goal of meditation. Theirs is true renunciation.

2 Therefore, Arjuna, you should understand that renunciation and the performance of selfless service are the same. Those who cannot renounce attachment to the results of their work are far from the path.

3 For aspirants who want to climb the mountain of spiritual awareness, the path is selfless work; for those who have ascended to yoga,

4 the path is stillness and peace. When a person has freed himself from attachment to the results of work, and from desires for the enjoyment of sense objects, he ascends to the unitive state.

5 Reshape yourself through the power of your will; never let yourself be degraded by self-will. The will is the only friend of the Self, and the will is the only enemy of the Self.

6 To those who have conquered themselves, the will is a friend. But it is the enemy of those who have not found the Self within them.

7 The supreme Reality stands revealed in the consciousness of those who have conquered themselves. They live in peace, alike in cold and heat, pleasure and pain, praise and blame.

8 They are completely fulfilled by spiritual wisdom and Self-realization. Having conquered their senses, they have climbed to the summit of human consciousness. To such people a clod of dirt, a stone, and gold are the same.

9 They are equally disposed to family, enemies, and friends, to those who support them and those who are hostile, to the good and the evil alike. Because they are impartial, they rise to great heights.

10 Those who aspire to the state of yoga should seek the Self in inner solitude through meditation. With body and mind controlled they should constantly practice one-pointedness, free from expectations and attachment to material possessions.

11 Select a clean spot, neither too high nor too low, and seat yourself firmly on a cloth, a
12 deerskin, and kusha grass. Then, once seated, strive to still your thoughts. Make your mind one-pointed in meditation, and your heart

13 will be purified. Hold your body, head, and neck firmly in a straight line, and keep your
14 eyes from wandering. With all fears dissolved in the peace of the Self and all desires dedicated to Brahman, controlling the mind and fixing it on me, sit in meditation with me as
15 your only goal. With senses and mind constantly controlled through meditation, united with the Self within, an aspirant attains nirvana, the state of abiding joy and peace in me.

16 Arjuna, those who eat too much or eat too little, who sleep too much or sleep too little,
17 will not succeed in meditation. But those who are temperate in eating and sleeping, work and recreation, will come to the end of
18 sorrow through meditation. Through constant effort they learn to withdraw the mind from selfish cravings and absorb it in the Self. Thus they attain the state of union.

19 When meditation is mastered, the mind is unwavering like the flame of a lamp in a
20 windless place. In the still mind, in the depths of meditation, the Self reveals itself. Beholding the Self by means of the Self, an aspirant knows the joy and peace of complete fulfill-
21 ment. Having attained that abiding joy beyond the senses, revealed in the stilled mind, he never swerves from the eternal
22 truth. He desires nothing else, and cannot be shaken by the heaviest burden of sorrow.

23 The practice of meditation frees one from all
affliction. This is the path of yoga. Follow
it with determination and sustained enthu-
24 siasm. Renouncing wholeheartedly all selfish
desires and expectations, use your will to
25 control the senses. Little by little, through
patience and repeated effort, the mind will
become stilled in the Self.

26 Wherever the mind wanders, restless and
diffuse in its search for satisfaction without,
27 lead it within; train it to rest in the Self. Abid-
ing joy comes to those who still the mind.
Freeing themselves from the taint of self-will,
with their consciousness unified, they become
one with Brahman.

28 The infinite joy of touching Brahman is easily
attained by those who are free from the burden
of evil and established within themselves.
29 They see the Self in every creature and all crea-
tion in the Self. With consciousness unified
through meditation, they see everything
with an equal eye.

30 I am ever present to those who have realized
me in every creature. Seeing all life as my
manifestation, they are never separated from
31 me. They worship me in the hearts of all, and
all their actions proceed from me. Wherever
they may live, they abide in me.

32 When a person responds to the joys and sorrows of others as if they were his own, he has attained the highest state of spiritual union.

ARJUNA:

33 O Krishna, the stillness of divine union which you describe is beyond my comprehension. How can the mind, which is so restless,
34 attain lasting peace? Krishna, the mind is restless, turbulent, powerful, violent; trying to control it is like trying to tame the wind.

SRI KRISHNA:

35 It is true that the mind is restless and difficult to control. But it can be conquered, Arjuna, through regular practice and detachment.
36 Those who lack self-control will find it difficult to progress in meditation; but those who are self-controlled, striving earnestly through the right means, will attain the goal.

ARJUNA:

37 Krishna, what happens to the man who has faith but who lacks self-control and wanders from the path, not attaining success in yoga?
38 If a man becomes deluded on the spiritual path, will he lose the support of both worlds,
39 like a cloud scattered in the sky? Krishna, you can dispel all doubts; remove this doubt which binds me.

SRI KRISHNA:

40 Arjuna, my son, such a person will not be destroyed. No one who does good work will ever come to a bad end, either here or in the world to come.

41 When such people die, they go to other realms where the righteous live. They dwell there for countless years and then are reborn into a

42 home which is pure and prosperous. Or they may be born into a family where meditation is practiced; to be born into such a family is

43 extremely rare. The wisdom they have acquired in previous lives will be reawakened, Arjuna, and they will strive even harder for

44 Self-realization. Indeed, they will be driven on by the strength of their past disciplines. Even one who inquires after the practice of meditation rises above those who simply perform rituals.

45 Through constant effort over many lifetimes, a person becomes purified of all selfish desires and attains the supreme goal of life.

46 Meditation is superior to severe asceticism and the path of knowledge. It is also superior to selfless service. May you attain the goal of

47 meditation, Arjuna! Even among those who meditate, that man or woman who worships me with perfect faith, completely absorbed in me, is the most firmly established in yoga.

Chapter 7
WISDOM FROM REALIZATION

1 With your mind intent on me, Arjuna, discipline yourself with the practice of yoga. Depend on me completely. Listen, and I will dispel all your doubts; you will come to know me fully and be united with me.

2 I will give you both jnana and vijnana. When both these are realized, there is nothing more you need to know.

3 One person in many thousands may seek perfection, yet of these only a few reach the
4 goal and come to realize me. Earth, water, fire, air, *akasha,* mind, intellect, and ego— these are the eight divisions of my prakriti.
5 But beyond this I have another, higher nature, Arjuna; it supports the whole universe and is the source of life in all beings.

6 In these two aspects of my nature is the womb of all creation. The birth and dissolution of the cosmos itself take place in me.
7 There is nothing that exists separate from me, Arjuna. The entire universe is suspended from me as my necklace of jewels.

8 Arjuna, I am the taste of pure water and the radiance of the sun and moon. I am the sacred word and the sound heard in air, and the cour-
9 age of human beings. I am the sweet fragrance in the earth and the radiance of fire; I am the life in every creature and the striving of the spiritual aspirant.

10 My eternal seed, Arjuna, is to be found in every creature. I am the power of discrimination in those who are intelligent, and the glory
11 of the noble. In those who are strong, I am strength, free from passion and selfish attachment. I am desire itself, if that desire is in harmony with the purpose of life.

12 The states of sattva, rajas, and tamas come
13 from me, but I am not in them. These three gunas deceive the world: people fail to look beyond them to me, supreme and imperish-
14 able. The three gunas make up my divine maya, difficult to overcome. But they cross
15 over this maya who take refuge in me. Others are deluded by maya; performing evil deeds, they have no devotion to me. Having lost all discrimination, they follow the way of their lower nature.

16 Good people come to worship me for different reasons. Some come to the spiritual life because of suffering, some in order to understand life; some come through a desire to

achieve life's purpose, and some come who
17 are men and women of wisdom. Unwavering
in devotion, always united with me, the man
or woman of wisdom surpasses all the others.
To them I am the dearest beloved, and they
18 are very dear to me. All those who follow the
spiritual path are blessed. But the wise who
are always established in union, for whom
there is no higher goal than me, may be re-
garded as my very Self.

19 After many births the wise seek refuge in
me, seeing me everywhere and in every-
20 thing. Such great souls are very rare. There
are others whose discrimination is misled by
many desires. Following their own nature,
they worship lower gods, practicing various
rites.

21 When a person is devoted to something with
22 complete faith, I unify his faith in that. Then,
when his faith is completely unified, he gains
the object of his devotion. In this way, every
23 desire is fulfilled by me. Those whose under-
standing is small attain only transient satisfac-
tion: those who worship the gods go to the
gods. But my devotees come to me.

24 Through lack of understanding, people
believe that I, the Unmanifest, have entered
into some form. They fail to realize my true
25 nature, which transcends birth and death. Few

see through the veil of maya. The world, de-
luded, does not know that I am without birth
26 and changeless. I know everything about the
past, the present, and the future, Arjuna; but
there is no one who knows me completely.

27 Delusion arises from the duality of attrac-
tion and aversion, Arjuna; every creature is
28 deluded by these from birth. But those who
have freed themselves from all wrongdoing
are firmly established in worship of me. Their
actions are pure, and they are free from the
delusion caused by the pairs of opposites.

29 Those who take refuge in me, striving for
liberation from old age and death, come to
know Brahman, the Self, and the nature of all
30 action. Those who see me ruling the cosmos,
who see me in the *adhibhuta,* the *adhidaiva,* and
the *adhiyajna,* are conscious of me even at the
time of death.

Chapter 8

THE ETERNAL GODHEAD

ARJUNA:

1 O Krishna, what is Brahman, and what is the
nature of action? What is the *adhyatma,* the
adhibhuta, the *adhidaiva?*

2 What is the *adhiyajna,* the supreme sacrifice,
and how is it to be offered? How are the self-
controlled united with you at the time of
death?

SRI KRISHNA:

3 My highest nature, the imperishable Brah-
man, gives every creature its existence and
lives in every creature as the adhyatma. My
action is creation and the bringing forth of
4 creatures. The adhibhuta is the perishable
body; the adhidaiva is Purusha, eternal spirit.
The adhiyajna, the supreme sacrifice, is made
to me as the Lord within you.

5 Those who remember me at the time of death
6 will come to me. Do not doubt this. Whatever
occupies the mind at the time of death deter-
mines the destination of the dying; always
they will tend toward that state of being.
7 Therefore, remember me at all times and fight

on. With your heart and mind intent on me,
8   you will surely come to me. When you make
your mind one-pointed through regular prac-
tice of meditation, you will find the supreme
glory of the Lord.

9   The Lord is the supreme poet, the first cause,
the sovereign ruler, subtler than the tiniest
particle, the support of all, inconceivable,
10   bright as the sun, beyond darkness. Remem-
bering him in this way at the time of death,
through devotion and the power of medita-
tion, with your mind completely stilled and
your concentration fixed in the center of
spiritual awareness between the eyebrows,
you will realize the supreme Lord.

11   I will tell you briefly of the eternal state all
scriptures affirm, which can be entered only
by those who are self-controlled and free from
selfish passions. Those whose lives are dedi-
cated to Brahman attain this supreme goal.

12   Remembering me at the time of death, close
down the doors of the senses and place the
mind in the heart. Then, while absorbed in
meditation, focus all energy upwards to the
13   head. Repeating in this state the divine Name,
the syllable *Om* that represents the changeless
Brahman, you will go forth from the body
and attain the supreme goal.

14 I am easily attained by the person who always
    remembers me and is attached to nothing else.

15 Such a person is a true yogi, Arjuna. Great
    souls make their lives perfect and discover me;
    they are freed from mortality and the suffer-

16 ing of this separate existence. Every creature
    in the universe is subject to rebirth, Arjuna,
    except the one who is united with me.

17 Those who understand the cosmic laws know
    that the day of Brahma ends after a thousand
    yugas and the night of Brahma ends after a

18 thousand yugas. When the day of Brahma
    dawns, forms are brought forth from the Un-
    manifest; when the night of Brahma comes,

19 these forms merge in the Formless again. This
    multitude of beings is created and destroyed
    again and again in the succeeding days and

20 nights of Brahma. But beyond this formless
    state there is another, unmanifested reality,
    which is eternal and is not dissolved when the

21 cosmos is destroyed. Those who realize life's
    supreme goal know that I am unmanifested
    and unchanging. Having come home to me,
    they never return to separate existence.

22 This supreme Lord who pervades all exis-
    tence, the true Self of all creatures, may be
    realized through undivided love.

23 There are two paths, Arjuna, which the soul
    may follow at the time of death. One leads to
    rebirth and the other to liberation.

24 The six months of the northern path of the
sun, the path of light, of fire, of day, of the
bright fortnight, leads knowers of Brahman
25 to the supreme goal. The six months of the
southern path of the sun, the path of smoke,
of night, of the dark fortnight, leads other
souls to the light of the moon and to rebirth.

26 These two paths, the light and the dark, are
said to be eternal, leading some to liberation
27 and others to rebirth. Once you have known
these two paths, Arjuna, you can never be de-
luded again. Attain this knowledge through
28 perseverance in yoga. There is merit in study-
ing the scriptures, in selfless service, austerity,
and giving, but the practice of meditation
carries you beyond all these to the supreme
abode of the highest Lord.

Chapter 9

THE ROYAL PATH

SRI KRISHNA:

1 Because of your faith, I shall tell you the most
profound of secrets: obtaining both jnana and
vijnana, you will be free from all evil.

2 This royal knowledge, this royal secret, is the
greatest purifier. Righteous and imperishable,
it is a joy to practice and can be directly experi-

3 enced. But those who have no faith in the
supreme law of life do not find me, Arjuna.
They return to the world, passing from death
to death.

4 I pervade the entire universe in my unmani-
fested form. All creatures find their existence

5 in me, but I am not limited by them. Behold
my divine mystery! These creatures do not
really dwell in me, and though I bring them
forth and support them, I am not confined

6 within them. They move in me as the winds
move in every direction in space.

7 At the end of the aeon these creatures return to
unmanifested matter; at the beginning of the

8 next cycle I send them forth again. Control-
ing my prakriti, again and again I bring forth

these myriad forms and subject them to the

9   laws of prakriti. None of these actions binds
me, Arjuna. I am unattached to them, so they
do not disturb my nature.

10 Under my watchful eye the laws of nature
take their couse. Thus is the world set in
motion; thus the animate and the inanimate
are created.

11 The foolish do not look beyond physical
appearances to see my true nature as the Lord

12 of all creation. The knowledge of such de-
luded people is empty; their lives are fraught
with disaster and evil and their work and
hopes are all in vain.

13 But truly great souls seek my divine nature.
They worship me with a one-pointed mind,
having realized that I am the eternal source of

14 all. Constantly striving, they make firm their
resolve and worship me without wavering.
Full of devotion, they sing of my divine
glory.

15 Others follow the path of jnana, spiritual wis-
dom. They see that where there is One, that
One is me; where there are many, all are me;
they see my face everywhere.

16 I am the ritual and the sacrifice; I am true
medicine and the *mantram*. I am the offering

and the fire which consumes it, and he to
whom it is offered.

17 I am the father and mother of this universe,
and its grandfather too; I am its entire sup-
port. I am the sum of all knowledge, the
purifier, the syllable *Om;* I am the sacred
scriptures, the Rik, Yajur, and Sama Vedas.

18 I am the goal of life, the Lord and support of
all, the inner witness, the abode of all. I am
the only refuge, the one true friend; I am the
beginning, the staying, and the end of
creation; I am the womb and the eternal seed.

19 I am heat; I give and withhold the rain. I am
immortality and I am death; I am what is and
what is not.

20 Those who follow the rituals given in the
Vedas, who offer sacrifices and take *soma,*
free themselves from evil and attain the vast
heaven of the gods, where they enjoy celestial
21 pleasures. When they have enjoyed these fully,
their merit is exhausted and they return to this
land of death. Thus observing Vedic rituals but
caught in an endless chain of desires, they
come and go.

22 Those who worship me and meditate on me
constantly, without any other thought, I will
provide for all their needs.

23 Those who worship other gods with faith and devotion also worship me, Arjuna, even if
24 they do not observe the usual forms. I am the object of all worship, its enjoyer and Lord. But those who fail to realize my true nature
25 must be reborn. Those who worship the devas will go to the realm of the devas; those who worship their ancestors will be united with them after death. Those who worship phantoms will become phantoms; but my devotees will come to me.

26 Whatever I am offered in devotion with a pure heart—a leaf, a flower, fruit, or water—
27 I partake of that love offering. Whatever you do, make it an offering to me—the food you eat, the sacrifices you make, the help you
28 give, even your suffering. In this way you will be freed from the bondage of karma, and from its results both pleasant and painful. Then, firm in renunciation and yoga, with your heart free, you will come to me.

29 I look upon all creatures equally; none is less dear to me and none more dear. But those who worship me with love live in me, and I come to life in them.

30 Even a sinner becomes holy when he worships me alone with firm resolve. Quickly his
31 soul conforms to dharma and he attains to boundless peace. Never forget this, Arjuna:

no one who is devoted to me will ever
come to harm.

32 All those who take refuge in me, whatever
their birth, race, sex, or caste, will attain the
supreme goal; this realization can be attained
33 even by those whom society scorns. Kings
and sages too seek this goal with devotion.
Therefore, having been born in this transient
and forlorn world, give all your love to me.
34 Fill your mind with me; love me; serve me;
worship me always. Seeking me in your
heart, you will at last be united with me.

Chapter 10

DIVINE SPLENDOR

SRI KRISHNA:

1 Listen further, Arjuna, to my supreme teaching, which gives you such joy. Desiring your welfare, O strong-armed warrior, I will tell you more.

2 Neither gods nor sages know my origin, for I am the source from which the gods and sages
3 come. Whoever knows me as the Lord of all creation, without birth or beginning, knows the truth and frees himself from all evil.

4 Discrimination, wisdom, understanding, forgiveness, truth, self-control, and peace of mind; pleasure and pain, birth and death, fear
5 and courage, honor and infamy; nonviolence, charity, equanimity, contentment, and perseverance in spiritual disciplines—all the different qualities found in living creatures have their source in me.

6 The seven great sages and the four ancient ancestors were born from my mind and re-
7 ceived my power. From them came all the creatures of this world. Whoever understands my

power and the mystery of my manifestations comes without doubt to be united with me.

8 I am the source from which all creatures evolve. The wise remember this and worship
9 me with loving devotion. Their thoughts are all absorbed in me, and all their vitality flows to me. Teaching one another, talking about me always, they are happy and fulfilled.

10 To those steadfast in love and devotion I give spiritual wisdom, so that they may come to
11 me. Out of compassion I destroy the darkness of their ignorance. From within them I light the lamp of wisdom and dispel all darkness from their lives.

ARJUNA:

12 You are Brahman supreme, the highest abode, the supreme purifier, the divine, eternal spirit, first among the gods, unborn
13 and infinite. The great sages and seers— Narada, Asita, Devala, and Vyasa too—have acclaimed you thus; now you have declared it to me yourself.

14 Now, O Krishna, I believe that everything you have told me is divine truth. O Lord, neither gods nor demons know your real
15 nature. Indeed, you alone know yourself, O supreme spirit. You are the source of

being and the master of every creature, God of gods, the Lord of the universe.

16 Tell me all your divine attributes, leaving nothing unsaid. Tell me of the glories with
17 which you fill the cosmos. Krishna, you are a supreme master of yoga. Tell me how I should meditate to gain constant awareness of you. In what things and in what ways should
18 I meditate on you? O Krishna, you who stir up people's hearts, tell me in detail your attributes and your powers; I can never tire of hearing your immortal words.

SRI KRISHNA:

19 All right, Arjuna, I will tell you of my divine powers. I will mention only the most glorious; for there is no end to them.

20 I am the true Self in the heart of every creature, Arjuna, and the beginning, middle, and end of their existence.

21 Among the shining gods I am Vishnu; of luminaries I am the sun; among the storm gods I am Marichi, and in the night sky I am the moon.

22 Among scriptures I am the Sama Veda, and among the lesser gods I am Indra. Among the senses I am the mind, and in living beings I am consciousness.

23 Among the Rudras I am Shankara. Among
the spirits of the natural world I am Kubera,
god of wealth, and Pavaka, the purifying fire.
Among mountains I am Meru.

24 Among priests I am Brihaspati, and among
military leaders I am Skanda. Among bodies
of water I am the ocean.

25 Among the great seers I am Bhrigu, and
among words, the syllable *Om;* I am the
repetition of the Holy Name, and among
mountains I am the Himalayas.

26 Among trees I am the *ashvattha,* the sacred fig;
among the *gandharvas* or heavenly musicians I
am Chitraratha. Among divine seers I am
Narada, and among sages I am Kapila.

27 I was born from the nectar of immortality
as the primordial horse and as Indra's noble
elephant. Among men, I am the king.

28 Among weapons I am the thunderbolt. I am
Kamadhuk, the cow that fulfills all desires; I
am Kandarpa, the power of sex, and Vasuki,
the king of snakes.

29 I am Ananta, the cosmic serpent, and Varuna,
the god of water; I am Aryaman among the
noble ancestors. Among the forces which
restrain I am Yama, the god of death.

30 Among animals I am the lion; among birds,
the eagle Garuda. I am Prahlada, born among
the demons, and of all that measures, I am
time.

31 Among purifying forces I am the wind;
among warriors, Rama. Of water creatures
I am the crocodile, and of rivers I am the
Ganges.

32 I am the beginning, middle, and end of crea-
tion. Of all the sciences I am the science of
Self-knowledge, and I am logic in those who
33 debate. Among letters I am *A;* among gram-
matical compounds I am the *dvandva*. I am
infinite time, and the sustainer whose face is
seen everywhere.

34 I am death, which overcomes all, and the
source of all beings still to be born. I am the
feminine qualities: fame, beauty, perfect
speech, memory, intelligence, loyalty, and
forgiveness.

35 Among the hymns of the Sama Veda I am the
Brihat; among poetic meters, the *gayatri*.
Among months I am Margashirsha, first of
the year; among seasons I am spring, that
brings forth flowers.

36 I am the gambling of the gambler and the
radiance in all that shines. I am effort, I am

victory, and I am the goodness of the
virtuous.

37 Among the Vrishnis I am Krishna, and
among the Pandavas I am Arjuna. Among
sages I am Vyasa, and among poets, Ushanas.

38 I am the scepter which metes out punishment,
and the art of statesmanship in those who
lead. I am the silence of the unknown and the
wisdom of the wise.

39 I am the seed that can be found in every
creature, Arjuna; for without me nothing
can exist, neither animate nor inanimate.

40 But there is no end to my divine attributes,
Arjuna; these I have mentioned are only a
41 few. Wherever you find strength, or beauty,
or spiritual power, you may be sure that these
have sprung from a spark of my essence.

42 But of what use is it to you to know all this,
Arjuna? Just remember that I am, and that I
support the entire cosmos with only a frag-
ment of my being.

Chapter 11
THE COSMIC VISION

ARJUNA:

1 Out of compassion you have taught me the
supreme mystery of the Self. Through your
2 words my delusion is gone. You have ex-
plained the origin and end of every creature,
O lotus-eyed one, and told me of your own
supreme, limitless existence.
3 Just as you have described your infinite
glory, O Lord, now I long to see it. I want to
4 see you as the supreme ruler of creation. O
Lord, master of yoga, if you think me strong
enough to behold it, show me your immortal
Self.

SRI KRISHNA:

5 Behold, Arjuna, a million divine forms, with
6 an infinite variety of color and shape. Behold
the gods of the natural world, and many more
7 wonders never revealed before. Behold the
entire cosmos turning within my body, and
the other things you desire to see.

8 But these things cannot be seen with your
physical eyes; therefore I give you spiritual
vision to perceive my majestic power.

SANJAYA:

9 Having spoken these words, Krishna, the
master of yoga, revealed to Arjuna his most
exalted, lordly form.

10 He appeared with an infinite number of faces,
ornamented by heavenly jewels, displaying
unending miracles and the countless weapons
11 of his power. Clothed in celestial garments
and covered with garlands, sweet-smelling
with heavenly fragrances, he showed himself
as the infinite Lord, the source of all wonders,
whose face is everywhere.

12 If a thousand suns were to rise in the heavens
at the same time, the blaze of their light
would resemble the splendor of that supreme
spirit.

13 There, within the body of the God of gods,
Arjuna saw all the manifold forms of the uni-
14 verse united as one. Filled with amazement,
his hair standing on end in ecstasy, he bowed
before the Lord with joined palms and spoke
these words.

ARJUNA:

15 O Lord, I see within your body all the
gods and every kind of living creature. I see
Brahma, the Creator, seated on a lotus; I see
the ancient sages and the celestial serpents.

16 I see infinite mouths and arms, stomachs and eyes, and you are embodied in every form. I see you everywhere, without beginning, middle, or end. You are the Lord of all creation, and the cosmos is your body.

17 You wear a crown and carry a mace and discus; your radiance is blinding and immeasurable. I see you, who are so difficult to behold, shining like a fiery sun blazing in every direction.

18 You are the supreme, changeless Reality, the one thing to be known. You are the refuge of all creation, the immortal spirit, the eternal guardian of eternal dharma.

19 You are without beginning, middle, or end; you touch everything with your infinite power. The sun and moon are your eyes, and your mouth is fire; your radiance warms the cosmos.

20 O Lord, your presence fills the heavens and the earth and reaches in every direction. I see the three worlds trembling before this vision of your wonderful and terrible form.

21 The gods enter your being, some calling out and greeting you in fear. Great saints sing your glory, praying, "May all be well!"

22 The multitudes of gods, demigods, and
    demons are all overwhelmed by the sight
23 of you. O mighty Lord, at the sight of your
    myriad eyes and mouths, arms and legs,
    stomachs and fearful teeth, I and the entire
    universe shake in terror.

24 O Vishnu, I can see your eyes shining; with
    open mouth, you glitter in an array of colors,
    and your body touches the sky. I look at you and
    my heart trembles; I have lost all courage
    and all peace of mind.

25 When I see your mouths with their fearful
    teeth, mouths burning like the fires at the end
    of time, I forget where I am and I have no
    place to go. O Lord, you are the support of
    the universe; have mercy on me!

26 I see all the sons of Dhritarashtra; I see Bhishma,
    Drona, and Karna; I see our warriors and
27 all the kings who are here to fight. All are
    rushing into your awful jaws; I see some of
28 them crushed by your teeth. As rivers flow
    into the ocean, all the warriors of this world
29 are passing into your fiery jaws; all creatures
    rush to their destruction like moths into a
    flame.

30 You lap the worlds into your burning mouths
    and swallow them. Filled with your terrible
    radiance. O Vishnu, the whole of creation
    bursts into flames.

31 Tell me who you are, O Lord of terrible
    form. I bow before you; have mercy! I want
    to know who you are, you who existed before
    all creation. Your nature and workings
    confound me.

SRI KRISHNA:

32 I am time, the destroyer of all; I have come
    to consume the world. Even without your
    participation, all the warriors gathered here
    will die.

33 Therefore arise, Arjuna; conquer your
    enemies and enjoy the glory of sovereignty.
    I have already slain all these warriors; you
    will only be my instrument.

34 Bhishma, Drona, Jayadratha, Karna, and
    many others are already slain. Kill those
    whom I have killed. Do not hesitate. Fight in
    this battle and you will conquer your enemies.

SANJAYA:

35 Having heard these words, Arjuna trembled
    in fear. With joined palms he bowed before
    Krishna and addressed him stammering.

ARJUNA:

36 O Krishna, it is right that the world delights
    and rejoices in your praise, that all the saints
    and sages bow down to you and all evil flees
    before you to the far corners of the universe.

37 How could they not worship you, O Lord?
You are the eternal spirit, who existed before
Brahma the Creator and who will never cease
to be. Lord of the gods, you are the abode
of the universe. Changeless, you are what is
and what is not, and beyond the duality of
existence and nonexistence.

38 You are the first among the gods, the timeless
spirit, the resting place of all beings. You are
the knower and the thing which is known.
You are the final home; with your infinite
form you pervade the cosmos.

39 You are Vayu, god of wind; Yama, god of
death; Agni, god of fire; Varuna, god of
water. You are the moon and the creator
Prajapati, and the great-grandfather of all
creatures. I bow before you and salute you
again and again.

40 You are behind me and in front of me;
I bow to you on every side. Your power is
immeasurable. You pervade everything;
you are everything.

41 Sometimes, because we were friends, I rashly
said, "Oh, Krishna!" "Say, friend!"—casual,
42 careless remarks. Whatever I may have said
lightly, whether we were playing or resting,
alone or in company, sitting together or eat-
ing, if it was disrespectful, forgive me for it,

O Krishna. I did not know the greatness of
your nature, unchanging and imperishable.

43 You are the father of the universe, of the ani-
mate and the inanimate; you are the object of
all worship, the greatest guru. There is none
to equal you in the three worlds. Who can
44 match your power? O gracious Lord, I
prostrate myself before you and ask for
your blessing. As a father forgives his son,
or a friend a friend, or a lover his beloved, so
should you forgive me.

45 I rejoice in seeing you as you have never been
seen before, yet I am filled with fear by this
vision of you as the abode of the universe.
Please let me see you again as the shining God
46 of all gods. Though you are the embodiment of
all creation, let me see you again not with a
thousand arms but with four, carrying the
mace and discus and wearing a crown.

SRI KRISHNA:

47 Arjuna, through my grace you have been
united with me and received this vision of my
radiant, universal form, without beginning
or end, which no one else has ever seen.

48 Not by knowledge of the Vedas, nor
sacrifice, nor charity, nor rituals, nor even
by severe asceticism has any other mortal
seen what you have seen, O heroic Arjuna.

49 Do not be troubled; do not fear my terrible
form. Let your heart be satisfied and your
fears dispelled in looking at me as I was
before.

SANJAYA:

50 Having spoken these words, the Lord once
again assumed the gentle form of Krishna and
consoled his devotee, who had been so afraid.

ARJUNA:

51 O Krishna, now that I have seen your gentle
human form my mind is again composed and
returned to normal.

SRI KRISHNA:

52 It is extremely difficult to obtain the vision
you have had; even the gods long always to
53 see me in this aspect. Neither knowledge of
the Vedas, nor austerity, nor charity, nor sac-
54 rifice can bring the vision you have seen. But
through unfailing devotion, Arjuna, you can
know me, see me, and attain union with me.
55 Whoever makes me the supreme goal of all
his work and acts without selfish attachment,
who devotes himself to me completely and is
free from ill will for any creature, enters into
me.

Chapter 12
THE WAY OF LOVE

ARJUNA:

1 Of those steadfast devotees who love you and
those who seek you as the eternal formless
Reality, who are the more established in yoga?

SRI KRISHNA:

2 Those who set their hearts on me and worship
me with unfailing devotion and faith are more
established in yoga.

3 As for those who seek the transcendental
Reality, without name, without form, con-
templating the Unmanifested, beyond the
4 reach of thought and of feeling, with their
senses subdued and mind serene and striving
for the good of all beings, they too will verily
come unto me.

5 Yet hazardous and slow is the path to the Un-
revealed, difficult for physical man to tread.
6 But they for whom I am the supreme goal,
who do all work renouncing self for me and
meditate on me with single-hearted devotion,
7 these I will swiftly rescue from the fragment's
cycle of birth and death, for their conscious-
ness has entered into me.

8 Still your mind in me, still your intellect in
me, and without doubt you will be united
9 with me forever. If you cannot still your mind
in me, learn to do so through the regular prac-
10 tice of meditation. If you lack the will for such
self-discipline, engage yourself in my work,
for selfless service can lead you at last to com-
11 plete fulfillment. If you are unable to do even
this, surrender yourself to me, disciplining
yourself and renouncing the results of all your
actions.

12 Better indeed is knowledge than mechanical
practice. Better than knowledge is medita-
tation. But better still is surrender of attachment
to results, because there follows immediate
peace.

13 That one I love who is incapable of ill will,
who is friendly and compassionate. Living
beyond the reach of *I* and *mine* and of pleasure
14 and pain, patient, contented, self-controlled,
firm in faith, with all his heart and all his mind
given to me—with such a one I am in love.

15 Not agitating the world or by it agitated, he
stands above the sway of elation, competi-
tion, and fear: he is my beloved.

16 He is detached, pure, efficient, impartial,
never anxious, selfless in all his undertakings;
he is my devotee, very dear to me.

17 He is dear to me who runs not after the pleasant or away from the painful, grieves not, lusts not, but lets things come and go as they happen.

18 That devotee who looks upon friend and foe with equal regard, who is not buoyed up by praise nor cast down by blame, alike in heat and cold, pleasure and pain, free from selfish *19* attachments, the same in honor and dishonor, quiet, ever full, in harmony everywhere, firm in faith—such a one is dear to me.

20 Those who meditate upon this immortal dharma as I have declared it, full of faith and seeking me as life's supreme goal, are truly my devotees, and my love for them is very great.

Chapter 13

THE FIELD AND THE KNOWER

SRI KRISHNA:

1   The body is called a field, Arjuna; he who
    knows it is called the Knower of the field.
    This is the knowledge of those who know.

2   I am the Knower of the field in everyone,
    Arjuna. Knowledge of the field and its
    Knower is true knowledge.

3   Listen and I will explain the nature of the field
    and how change takes place within it. I will
    also describe the Knower of the field and his

4   power. These truths have been sung by great
    sages in a variety of ways, and expounded in
    precise arguments concerning Brahman.

5   The field, Arjuna, is made up of the follow-
    ing: the five areas of sense perception; the five
    elements; the five sense organs and the five
    organs of action; the three components of the
    mind: *manas, buddhi,* and *ahamkara*; and the
    undifferentiated energy from which all these

6   evolved. In this field arise desire and aversion,
    pleasure and pain, the body, intelligence, and
    will.

7   Those who know truly are free from pride
    and deceit. They are gentle, forgiving, up-

right, and pure, devoted to their spiritual
teacher, filled with inner strength, and self-
8 controlled. Detached from sense objects and
self-will, they have learned the painful lesson
of separate birth and suffering, old age,
disease, and death.

9 Free from selfish attachment, they do not get
compulsively entangled even in home and
family. They are even-minded through good
10 fortune and bad. Their devotion to me is un-
divided. Enjoying solitude and not following
11 the crowd, they seek only me. This is true
knowledge, to seek the Self as the true end
of wisdom always. To seek anything else is
ignorance.

12 I will tell you of the wisdom that leads to im-
mortality: the beginningless Brahman, which
can be called neither being nor nonbeing.

13 It dwells in all, in every hand and foot and
head, in every mouth and eye and ear in the
14 universe. Without senses itself, it shines
through the functioning of the senses. Com-
pletely independent, it supports all things.
Beyond the gunas, it enjoys their play.

15 It is both near and far, both within and with-
out every creature; it moves and is unmoving.
16 In its subtlety it is beyond comprehension. It
is indivisible, yet appears divided in separate

creatures. Know it to be the creator, the pre-
server, and the destroyer.

17 Dwelling in every heart, it is beyond darkness.
It is called the light of lights, the object and goal
of knowledge, and knowledge itself.

18 I have revealed to you the nature of the field
and the meaning and object of true knowledge.
Those who are devoted to me, knowing these
things, are united with me.

19 Know that prakriti and Purusha are both
without beginning, and that from prakriti come
20 the gunas and all that changes. Prakriti is the
agent, cause, and effect of every action, but
it is Purusha that seems to experience pleasure
and pain.

21 Purusha, resting in prakriti, witnesses the
play of the gunas born of prakriti. But attach-
ment to the gunas leads a person to be born
for good or evil.

22 Within the body the supreme Purusha is called
the witness, approver, supporter, enjoyer, the
supreme Lord, the highest Self.

23 Whoever realizes the true nature of Purusha,
prakriti, and the gunas, whatever path he or
she may follow, is not born separate again.

24 Some realize the Self within them through the practice of meditation, some by the path of wisdom, and others by selfless service.

25 Others may not know these paths; but hearing and following the instructions of an illumined teacher, they too go beyond death.

26 Whatever exists, Arjuna, animate or inanimate, is born through the union of the field and its Knower.

27 He alone sees truly who sees the Lord the same in every creature, who sees the Death-

28 less in the hearts of all that die. Seeing the same Lord everywhere, he does not harm himself or others. Thus he attains the supreme goal.

29 They alone see truly who see that all actions are performed by prakriti, while the Self re-

30 mains unmoved. When they see the variety of creation rooted in that unity and growing out of it, they attain fulfillment in Brahman.

31 This supreme Self is without a beginning, undifferentiated, deathless. Though it dwells in the body, Arjuna, it neither acts nor is

32 touched by action. As *akasha* pervades the cosmos but remains unstained, the Self can never be tainted though it dwells in every creature.

33 As the sun lights up the world, the Self dwell-
ing in the field is the source of all light in the
34 field. Those who, with the eye of wisdom,
distinguish the field from its Knower and
the way to freedom from the bondage of
prakriti, attain the supreme goal.

Chapter 14
THE FORCES OF EVOLUTION

1 Let me tell you more about the wisdom that
transcends all knowledge, through which the
2 saints and sages attained perfection. Those
who rely on this wisdom will be united with
me. For them there is neither rebirth nor fear
of death.

3 My womb is prakriti; in that I place the seed.
4 Thus all created things are born. Everything
born, Arjuna, comes from the womb of
prakriti, and I am the seed-giving father.

5 It is the three gunas born of prakriti—sattva,
rajas, and tamas—that bind the immortal Self
6 to the body. Sattva—pure, luminous, and free
from sorrow—binds us with attachment to
7 happiness and wisdom. Rajas is passion, aris-
ing from selfish desire and attachment. These
8 bind the Self with compulsive action. Tamas,
born of ignorance, deludes all creatures
through heedlessness, indolence, and sleep.

9 Sattva binds us to happiness; rajas binds us to
action. Tamas, distorting our understanding,
binds us to delusion.

10 Sattva predominates when rajas and tamas
are transformed. Rajas prevails when sattva
is weak and tamas overcome. Tamas prevails
when rajas and sattva are dormant.

11 When sattva predominates, the light of wis-
dom shines through every gate of the body.
12 When rajas predominates, a person runs about
pursuing selfish and greedy ends, driven by
13 restlessness and desire. When tamas is domi-
nant a person lives in darkness—slothful, con-
fused, and easily infatuated.

14 Those dying in the state of sattva attain the
15 pure worlds of the wise. Those dying in rajas
are reborn among people driven by work. But
those who die in tamas are conceived in the
wombs of the ignorant.

16 The fruit of good deeds is pure and sattvic.
The fruit of rajas is suffering. The fruit of
tamas is ignorance and insensitivity.

17 From sattva comes understanding; from rajas,
greed. But the outcome of tamas is confusion,
infatuation, and ignorance.

18 Those who live in sattva go upwards; those
in rajas remain where they are. But those
immersed in tamas sink downwards.

19 The wise see clearly that all action is the work of the gunas. Knowing that which is above the gunas, they enter into union with me.

20 Going beyond the three gunas which form the body, they leave behind the cycle of birth and death, decrepitude and sorrow, and attain to immortality.

ARJUNA:

21 What are the characteristics of those who have gone beyond the gunas, O Lord? How do they act? How have they passed beyond the gunas' hold?

SRI KRISHNA:

22 They are unmoved by the harmony of sattva, the activity of rajas, or the delusion of tamas. They feel no aversion when these forces are active, nor do they crave for them when these forces subside.

23 They remain impartial, undisturbed by the actions of the gunas. Knowing that it is the gunas which act, they abide within themselves and do not vacillate.

24 Established within themselves, they are equal in pleasure and pain, praise and blame, kindness and unkindness. Clay, a rock, and gold
25 are the same to them. Alike in honor and dishonor, alike to friend and foe, they have

given up every selfish pursuit. Such are those who have gone beyond the gunas.

26 By serving me with steadfast love, a man or woman goes beyond the gunas. Such a one is fit for union with Brahman. For I am the support of Brahman, the eternal, the unchanging, the deathless, the everlasting dharma, the source of all joy.

Chapter 15

THE SUPREME SELF

SRI KRISHNA:

1 Sages speak of the immutable *ashvattha* tree,
with its taproot above and its branches below.
On this tree grow the scriptures; seeing their
source, one knows their essence.

2 Nourished by the gunas, the limbs of this tree
spread above and below. Sense objects grow
on the limbs as buds; the roots hanging down
bind us to action in this world.

3 The true form of this tree—its essence,
beginning, and end—is not perceived on this
earth. Cut down this strong-rooted tree with
4 the sharp ax of detachment; then find the
path which does not come back again. Seek
that, the First Cause, from which the uni-
verse came long ago.

5 Not deluded by pride, free from selfish
attachment and selfish desire, beyond the
duality of pleasure and pain, ever aware of the
Self, the wise go forward to that eternal goal.
6 Neither the sun nor the moon nor fire can
add to that light. This is my supreme abode,

and those who enter there do not return to
separate existence.

7 An eternal part of me enters into the world,
assuming the powers of action and percep-
8 tion and a mind made of prakriti. When
the divine Self enters and leaves a body, it
takes these along as the wind carries a scent
9 from place to place. Using the mind, ears,
eyes, nose, and the senses of taste and touch,
the Self enjoys sense objects.

10 The deluded do not see the Self when it leaves
the body or when it dwells within it. They
do not see the Self enjoying sense objects or
acting through the guna. But they who have
the eye of wisdom see.

11 Those who strive resolutely on the path of
yoga see the Self within. The thoughtless,
who strive imperfectly, do not.

12 The brightness of the sun, which lights up
the world, the brightness of the moon and
13 of fire—these are my glory. With a drop of
my energy I enter the earth and support all
creatures. Through the moon, the vessel of
14 life-giving fluid, I nourish all plants. I enter
breathing creatures and dwell within as the
life-giving breath. I am the fire in the stomach
which digests all food.

15 Entering into every heart, I give the power
to remember and understand; it is I again who
take that power away. All the scriptures lead
to me; I am their author and their wisdom.

16 In this world there are two orders of being:
the perishable, separate creature and the
17 changeless spirit. But beyond these there is
another, the supreme Self, the eternal Lord,
who enters into the entire cosmos and
supports it from within.

18 I am that supreme Self, praised by the scrip-
tures as beyond the changing and the change-
19 less. Those who see in me that supreme Self
see truly. They have found the source of all
wisdom, Arjuna, and they worship me with
all their heart.

20 I have shared this profound truth with you,
Arjuna. Those who understand it will attain
wisdom; they will have done that which has
to be done.

Chapter 16
TWO PATHS

1 Be fearless and pure; never waver in your de-
termination or your dedication to the spiritual
life. Give freely. Be self-controlled, sincere,
truthful, loving, and full of the desire to serve.
Realize the truth of the scriptures; learn to be
2 detached and to take joy in renunciation. Do
not get angry or harm any living creature, but
be compassionate and gentle; show goodwill
3 to all. Cultivate vigor, patience, will, purity;
avoid malice and pride. Then, Arjuna, you
will achieve your divine destiny.

4 Other qualities, Arjuna, make a person more
and more inhuman: hypocrisy, arrogance,
conceit, anger, cruelty, ignorance.

5 The divine qualities lead to freedom; the
demonic, to bondage. But do not grieve,
Arjuna; you were born with divine attributes.

6 Some people have divine tendencies, others
demonic. I have described the divine at
length, Arjuna; now listen while I describe
the demonic.

7 The demonic do things they should avoid and
avoid the things they should do. They have
no sense of uprightness, purity, or truth.

8 "There is no God," they say, "no truth, no
spiritual law, no moral order. The basis of life
9 is sex; what else can it be?" Holding such dis-
torted views, possessing scant discrimination,
they become enemies of the world, causing
suffering and destruction.

10 Hypocritical, proud, and arrogant, living in
delusion and clinging to deluded ideas, insatia-
ble in their desires, they pursue their unclean
11 ends. Although burdened with fears that end
only with death, they still maintain with com-
plete assurance, "Gratification of lust is the
highest that life can offer."

12 Bound on all sides by scheming and anxiety,
driven by anger and greed, they amass by any
means they can a hoard of money for the
satisfaction of their cravings.

13 "I got this today," they say; "tomorrow I
shall get that. This wealth is mine, and that
14 will be mine too. I have destroyed my ene-
mies. I shall destroy others too! Am I not like
God? I enjoy what I want. I am successful. I
15 am powerful. I am happy. I am rich and well-
born. Who is equal to me? I will perform sac-

rifices and give gifts, and rejoice in my own
generosity." This is how they go on, deluded
16 by ignorance. Bound by their greed and en-
tangled in a web of delusion, whirled about
by a fragmented mind, they fall into a dark
hell.

17 Self-important, obstinate, swept away by the
pride of wealth, they ostentatiously perform
sacrifices without any regard for their pur-
18 pose. Egotistical, violent, arrogant, lustful,
angry, envious of everyone, they abuse my
presence within their own bodies and in the
bodies of others.

19 Life after life I cast those who are malicious,
hateful, cruel, and degraded into the wombs
20 of those with similar demonic natures. Birth
after birth they find themselves with demonic
tendencies. Degraded in this way, Arjuna,
they fail to reach me and fall lower still.

21 There are three gates to this self-destructive
hell: lust, anger, and greed. Renounce these
22 three. Those who escape from these three
gates of darkness, Arjuna, seek what is best
23 and attain life's supreme goal. Others dis-
regard the teachings of the scriptures. Driven
by selfish desire, they miss the goal of life,
miss even happiness and success.

24 Therefore let the scriptures be your guide in what to do and what not to do. Understand their teachings; then act in accordance with them.

Chapter 17
THE POWER OF FAITH

ARJUNA:

1 O Krishna, what is the state of those who disregard the scriptures but still worship with faith? Do they act from sattava, rajas, or tamas?

SRI KRISHNA:

2 Every creature is born with faith of some kind, either sattvic, rajasic, or tamasic. Listen, and I will describe each to you.

3 Our faith conforms to our nature, Arjuna. Human nature is made of faith. Indeed, a person is his faith.

4 Those who are sattvic worship the forms of God; those who are rajasic worship power and wealth. Those who are tamasic worship

5 spirits and ghosts. Some invent harsh penances. Motivated by hypocrisy and egotism,

6 they torture their innocent bodies and me who dwells within. Blinded by their strength and passion, they act and think like demons.

7 The three kinds of faith express themselves in the habits of those who hold them: in the food they like, the work they do, the disciplines

they practice, the gifts they give. Listen, and I
will describe their different ways.

8 Sattvic people enjoy food that is mild, tasty,
substantial, agreeable, and nourishing, food
that promotes health, strength, cheerfulness,
9 and longevity. Rajasic people like food that is
salty or bitter, hot, sour, or spicy—food that
promotes pain, discomfort, and disease.
10 Tamasic people like overcooked, stale, left-
over, and impure food, food that has lost its
taste and nutritional value.

11 The sattvic perform sacrifices with their entire
mind fixed on the purpose of the sacrifice.
Without thought of reward, they follow the
12 teachings of the scriptures. The rajasic per-
form sacrifices for the sake of show and the
13 good it will bring them. The tamasic perform
sacrifices ignoring both the letter and the
spirit. They omit the proper prayers, the
proper offerings, the proper food, and the
proper faith.

14 To offer service to the gods, to the good, to
the wise, and to your spiritual teacher; purity,
honesty, continence, and nonviolence: these
15 are the disciplines of the body. To offer sooth-
ing words, to speak truly, kindly, and helpful-
ly, and to study the scriptures: these are the
16 disciplines of speech. Calmness, gentleness,

silence, self-restraint, and purity: these are the disciplines of the mind.

17 When these three levels of self-discipline are practiced without attachment to the results, but in a spirit of great faith, the sages call this

18 practice sattvic. Disciplines practiced in order to gain respect, honor, or admiration are rajasic; they are undependable and transitory

19 in their effects. Disciplines practiced to gain power over others, or in the confused belief that to torture oneself is spiritual, are tamasic.

20 Giving simply because it is right to give, without thought of return, at a proper time, in proper circumstances, and to a worthy per-

21 son, is sattvic giving. Giving with regrets or in the expectation of receiving some favor or of

22 getting something in return is rajasic. Giving at an inappropriate time, in inappropriate circumstances, and to an unworthy person, without affection or respect, is tamasic.

23 *Om Tat Sat:* these three words represent Brahman, from which come priests and

24 scriptures and sacrifice. Those who follow the Vedas, therefore, always repeat the word *Om* when offering sacrifices, performing spiritual

25 disciplines, or giving gifts. Those seeking liberation and not any personal benefit add the word *Tat* when performing these acts

26 of worship, discipline, and charity. *Sat*
means "that which is"; it also indicates good-
ness. Therefore it is used to describe a worthy
deed.

27 To be steadfast in self-sacrifice, self-discipline,
and giving is *sat.* To act in accordance with
28 these three is *sat* as well. But to engage in sac-
rifice, self-discipline, and giving without
good faith is *asat,* without worth or goodness,
either in this life or in the next.

Chapter 18

FREEDOM AND RENUNCIATION

ARJUNA:

1 O Krishna, destroyer of evil, please explain to me *sannyasa* and *tyaga* and how one kind of renunciation differs from another.

SRI KRISHNA:

2 To refrain from selfish acts is one kind of renunciation, called sannyasa; to renounce the fruit of action is another, called tyaga.

3 Among the wise, some say that all action should be renounced as evil. Others say that certain kinds of action—self-sacrifice, giving,

4 and self-discipline—should be continued. Listen, Arjuna, and I will explain three kinds of tyaga and my conclusions concerning them.

5 Self-sacrifice, giving, and self-discipline should not be renounced, for they purify the

6 thoughtful. Yet even these, Arjuna, should be performed without desire for selfish rewards. This is essential.

7 To renounce one's responsibilities is not fitting. The wise call such deluded renuncia-

8 tion tamasic. To avoid action from fear of dif-

ficulty or physical discomfort is rajasic. There
9 is no reward in such renunciation. But to
fulfill your responsibilities knowing that they
are obligatory, while at the same time desiring
nothing for yourself—this is sattvic renuncia-
10 tion. Those endowed with sattva clearly
understand the meaning of renunciation and
do not waver. They are not intimidated by
unpleasant work, nor do they seek a job
because it is pleasant.

11 As long as one has a body, one cannot re-
nounce action altogether. True renunciation
is giving up all desire for personal reward.
12 Those who are attached to personal reward
will reap the consequences of their actions:
some pleasant, some unpleasant, some mixed.
But those who renounce every desire for per-
sonal reward go beyond the reach of karma.

13 Listen, Arjuna, and I will explain the five
elements necessary for the accomplishment
of every action, as taught by the wisdom of
14 Sankhya. The body, the means, the ego, the
performance of the act, and the divine will:
15 these are the five factors in all actions, right
or wrong, in thought, word, or deed.

16 Those who do not understand this think of
themselves as separate agents. With their
crude intellects they fail to see the truth.
17 The person who is free from ego, who has

attained purity of heart, though he slays these
people, he does not slay and is not bound by
his action.

18 Knowledge, the thing to be known, and
    the knower: these three promote action. The
    means, the act itself, and the doer: these three
19 are the totality of action. Knowledge, action,
    and the doer can be described according to the
    gunas. Listen, and I will explain their distinc-
    tions to you.

20 Sattvic knowledge sees the one indestructi-
    ble Being in all beings, the unity underlying
21 the multiplicity of creation. Rajasic knowl-
    edge sees all things and creatures as separate
22 and distinct. Tamasic knowledge, lacking
    any sense of perspective, sees one small
    part and mistakes it for the whole.

23 Work performed to fulfill one's obligations,
    without thought of personal reward or of
    whether the job is pleasant or unpleasant, is
24 sattvic. Work prompted by selfish desire or
25 self-will, full of stress, is rajasic. Work that is
    undertaken blindly, without any considera-
    tion of consequences, waste, injury to others,
    or one's own capacities, is tamasic.

26 A sattvic worker is free from egotism and
    selfish attachments, full of enthusiasm and
27 fortitude in success and failure alike. A rajasic

worker has strong personal desires and craves
rewards for his actions. Covetous, impure,
and destructive, he is easily swept away by
28 fortune, good or bad. The tamasic worker is
undisciplined, vulgar, stubborn, deceitful,
dishonest, and lazy. He is easily depressed and
prone to procrastination.

29 Listen, Arjuna, as I describe the three types of
understanding and will.

30 To know when to act and when to refrain
from action, what is right action and what
is wrong, what brings security and what in-
security, what brings freedom and what bond-
age: these are the signs of a sattvic intellect.

31 The rajasic intellect confuses right and wrong
actions, and cannot distinguish what is to be
32 done from what should not be done. The
tamasic intellect is shrouded in darkness,
utterly reversing right and wrong wherever
it turns.

33 The sattvic will, developed through medita-
tion, keeps *prana,* mind, and senses in vital
34 harmony. The rajasic will, conditioned by
selfish desire, pursues wealth, pleasure, and
35 respectability. The tamasic will shows itself
in obstinate ignorance, sloth, fear, grief,
depression, and conceit.

36 Now listen, Arjuna: there are also three kinds
of happiness. By sustained effort, one comes
to the end of sorrow.

37 That which seems like poison at first, but
tastes like nectar in the end—this is the joy of
sattva, born of a mind at peace with itself.

38 Pleasure from the senses seems like nectar at
first, but it is bitter as poison in the end. This
is the kind of happiness that comes to the

39 rajasic. Those who are tamasic draw their
pleasures from sleep, indolence, and intoxi-
cation. Both in the beginning and in the end,
this happiness is a delusion.

40 No creature, whether born on earth or among
the gods in heaven, is free from the

41 conditioning of the three gunas. The different
responsibilities found in the social order—dis-
tinguishing brahmin, kshatriya, vaishya, and
shudra—have their roots in this conditioning.

42 The responsibilities to which a brahmin is
born, based on his nature, are self-control,
tranquillity, purity of heart, patience, humil-
ity, learning, austerity, wisdom, and faith.

43 The qualities of a kshatriya, based on his
nature, are courage, strength, fortitude,
dexterity, generosity, leadership, and the

44 firm resolve never to retreat from battle. The
occupations suitable for a vaishya are agricul-

ture, dairying, and trade. The proper work of
a shudra is service.

45 By devotion to one's own particular duty,
everyone can attain perfection. Let me tell
46 you how. By performing his own work, one
worships the Creator who dwells in every
creature. Such worship brings that person to
fulfillment.

47 It is better to perform one's own duties im-
perfectly than to master the duties of another.
By fulfilling the obligations he is born with, a
48 person never comes to grief. No one should
abandon duties because he sees defects in
them. Every action, every activity, is sur-
rounded by defects as a fire is surrounded by
smoke.

49 He who is free from selfish attachments, who
has mastered himself and his passions, attains
the supreme perfection of freedom from ac-
50 tion. Listen and I shall explain now, Arjuna,
how one who has attained perfection also
attains Brahman, the supreme consummation
of wisdom.

51 Unerring in his discrimination, sovereign of
his senses and passions, free from the clamor
52 of likes and dislikes, he leads a simple, self-
reliant life based on meditation, controlling
his speech, body, and mind.

53 Free from self-will, aggressiveness, arro-
gance, anger, and the lust to possess people or
things, he is at peace with himself and others

54 and enters into the unitive state. United with
Brahman, ever joyful, beyond the reach of de-
sire and sorrow, he has equal regard for every
living creature and attains supreme devotion

55 to me. By loving me he comes to know me
truly; then he knows my glory and enters

56 into my boundless being. All his acts are
performed in my service, and through my
grace he wins eternal life.

57 Make every act an offering to me; regard me
as your only protector. Relying on interior

58 discipline, meditate on me always. Remember-
ing me, you shall overcome all difficulties
through my grace. But if you will not heed
me in your self-will, nothing will avail you.

59 If you egotistically say, "I will not fight this
battle," your resolve will be useless; your

60 own nature will drive you into it. Your own
karma, born of your own nature, will drive
you to do even that which you do not wish
to do, because of your delusion.

61 The Lord dwells in the hearts of all creatures
and whirls them round upon the wheel of

62 maya. Run to him for refuge with all your
strength, and peace profound will be yours
through his grace.

63 I give you these precious words of wisdom;
reflect on them and then do as you choose.

64 These are the last words I shall speak to you,
dear one, for your spiritual fulfillment. You
are very dear to me.

65 Be aware of me always, adore me, make
every act an offering to me, and you shall
come to me; this I promise; for you are dear

66 to me. Abandon all supports and look to me
for protection. I shall purify you from the
sins of the past; do not grieve.

67 Do not share this wisdom with anyone who
lacks in devotion or self-control, lacks the de-

68 sire to learn, or scoffs at me. Those who teach
this supreme mystery of the Gita to all who
love me perform the greatest act of love; they

69 will come to me without doubt. No one can
render me more devoted service; no one on
earth can be more dear to me.

70 Those who meditate on these holy words
71 worship me with wisdom and devotion. Even
those who listen to them with faith, free from
doubts, will find a happier world where good
people dwell.

72 Have you listened with attention? Are you
now free from your doubts and confusion?

ARJUNA:

73 You have dispelled my doubts and delusions,
and I understand through your grace. My
faith is firm now, and I will do your will.

SANJAYA:

74 This is the dialogue I heard between Krishna,
the son of Vasudeva, and Arjuna, the great-
hearted son of Pritha. The wonder of it makes
75 my hair stand on end! Through Vyasa's grace,
I have heard the supreme secret of spiritual
union directly from the Lord of Yoga,
Krishna himself.

76 Whenever I remember these wonderful,
holy words between Krishna and Arjuna, I
77 am filled with joy. And when I remember the
breathtaking form of Krishna, I am filled with
wonder and my joy overflows.

78 Wherever the divine Krishna and the mighty
Arjuna are, there will be prosperity, victory,
happiness, and sound judgment. Of this I am
sure!

NOTES

CHAPTER ONE

1 The phrase "the field of dharma" (*dharma-kshetra*)
gives a hint that the battle is to be an allegorical one, a
fight of *dharma,* justice, against *adharma,* evil. The bat-
tle takes place not only at Kurukshetra, the "field of the
Kurus," but also on the elusive "field of dharma," the
spiritual realm where all moral struggles are waged.

40–44 These verses are particularly difficult to translate,
because they revolve around the complex word
dharma: law, justice, or simply something's inner
nature. To try to capture the word in English we
might say "God's law" or "eternal truth." Dharma is
divinely given; it is the force that holds things together
in a unity, the center that must hold if all is to go well.
The opposite of dharma is *adharma*: evil, injustice,
chaos. In these verses Arjuna gives expression to his
fears of a coming chaos, an evil world where good
people will be confused and violated. "Sense of unity"
here translates *dharma*; the phrase "loses its sense of
unity" would be more literally translated as "is over-
come by *adharma*."

The translation speaks in a general way of the chaos

that overcomes society when dharma is weak—when ancient spiritual truths are ignored. Thus *varna-samkara,* literally "confusion of caste," is more meaningful as "society [is] plunged into chaos." The subject here is not the observance of caste restrictions but the essential cohesion of the social fabric.

42 The Sanskrit refers to the ancient *pinda* rites that offer homage to dead ancestors. These rites maintained the traditions of the family by respecting and worshiping those who had gone before. Again, the rather liberal rendering "spiritual evolution begun by our ancestors" seems preferable to a narrower translation.

CHAPTER TWO

17 *Tat,* "that," is an ancient name for Brahman, the supreme reality. Brahman is neither masculine nor feminine; in fact, it has no attributes at all. It is impossible to describe Brahman in words, so it is simply pointed to: *tat.*

72 The state of immortality is *brahmanirvana,* "the nirvana that is Brahman." This is the state of release or liberation, union with the divine ground of existence. The word *nirvana* comes from the Sanskrit root *va,* "to blow," with the prefix *nir,* "out"; it means "to extinguish," as a fire is said to be "blown out." Thus it indicates the extinction of the old, limited personality. By adding the word *brahman,* complete union with the universal Godhead is indicated. *Brahmanirvana* then means the mystic state of extinction of self in the union with God. *Nirvana* is a Buddhist term as well, and Buddhist definitions have generally received more attention in the English-speaking world. Because of the austere nature of Buddhist discourse, some mis-

conceptions are unfortunately current about this rather esoteric concept. Nirvana is wrongly presented as a kind of empty nothingness, even a spiritual death. We get exactly the opposite impression if we approach the Hindus and Buddhists themselves. It is true there is much talk of extinguishing the petty ego and going beyond self-will, but this is just to say that it is necessary to jettison the limited, weak personality—the mask that hides the creative, wise, loving Self underneath. This "death" of the old man to make way for the new is one purpose of spiritual disciplines. It can be painful, but the death of the old man leads not to annihilation but to a spiritual rebirth.

CHAPTER THREE

9 Here and later *yajna* is translated as "selfless work" or "selfless service." The literal meaning is sacrifice: essentially, self-sacrifice, giving up something one greatly values for the sake of a higher purpose. Some translators give a very narrow translation of *yajna* as a ritualistic sacrifice, but this is inaccurate. The Gita is not at all concerned with ritual religion and in fact deprecates it quite a few times.

39 *Kama* can be translated as selfish desire or pleasure, and often carries a connotation of sensual desire or sexual passion. It means essentially a personal desire for ease or pleasure, not "desire" of a more altruistic kind.

CHAPTER FOUR

37 This is a well-known verse. The meanings of *karma* are complex, but the verse is widely taken to mean that true knowledge destroys the effects of past errors,

which generate further karma. When consciousness is unified and illumined, one is released from the bondage of karma.

CHAPTER FIVE

6 *Yoga* has many meanings in the Gita, some of which are discussed in the preface. Here *yoga* is translated as "action" and "selfless service" because a contrast is being made between Sankhya and yoga: that is, between philosophical explanation and the actual practice of the spiritual life.

9 The word for "senses" in Sanskrit is *indriya,* literally "faculty" or "power." The indriyas are not only the five faculties of perception (seeing, hearing, touching, smelling, and tasting) but also those of action, whose organs are the hands, the feet, the tongue, and the organs of excretion and reproduction.

13 "The city of nine gates" is the body. The gates are the two eyes, the two nostrils, the two ears, the mouth, and the organs of excretion and reproduction. In some lists these gates are expanded to eleven by adding the navel and the *brahmarandhra* or sagittal suture, the opening at the top of the skull.

27–28 The "center of spiritual consciousness" is one of the seven centers of awareness or *chakras* described in yoga literature. These seven chakras, though not physical, are said to lie along a channel for awakened spiritual energy (*kundalini*) that corresponds with the spine; the chakras are located at the level of the anus, sex organs, stomach, heart, throat, eyebrows, and the top of the head. Kundalini circulates among these centers, but it is usually confined to the lowest three chakras, corresponding to the main preoccupations of life on the physical level. In yogic concentration the vital energy (kundalini) rises: samadhi is said to take place when it reaches the chakras at the brow or head.

CHAPTER SIX

11 This stanza describes the traditional seat used for meditation. The Gita is not concerned with the outer forms of the spiritual life, but here we do get a mention of the grass and deerskin used by the ancient sages. Perhaps the point is that they used what was available in their forest retreats, and that the seat should be what Patanjali calls *sukhasana*: comfortable enough to forget about your body, not so comfortable that you fall asleep.

14 "All desires dedicated to Brahman" is a literal translation of the Sanskrit word *brahmacharya*, a life of self-control and sense restraint.

CHAPTER SEVEN

16 *Artharthi* has given translators some difficulties. "Those who desire to achieve life's purpose" captures the basic meaning of the word. *Artha* is goal or purpose; the second word of the compound, *arthi*, means "one who has a goal." So *artharthi* probably refers to those who take to the spiritual life with a particular purpose in view. *Artha* also means wealth or worldly goods, but to translate this phrase as "those who desire wealth" would go against the entire tenor of the Gita.

23 "Lower gods" here refers to the *devas*, the lower, celestial deities such as Indra.

30 These obscure terms (*adhibhuta, adhidaiva,* and *adhiyajna*) are taken up in the next chapter.

CHAPTER EIGHT

6 "Whatever occupies the mind at the time of death" determines the direction of the soul's rebirth. The implication is that whatever has been the bedrock of consciousness during life will be remembered at the time of death and lead the soul on to fulfill that desire in the next life.

10 The "center of spiritual awareness between the eyebrows" is discussed in the note to 5:27–28.

CHAPTER NINE

5 *Yoga* here means "mysterious power." This is yet another meaning attached to the word *yoga,* for those who practiced yoga were sometimes thought of as concealing within themselves extraordinary powers developed through their disciplines. The folklore of India relates many stories about mysterious holy men who have strange, divine powers.

Krishna speaks here of his *yoga aishvaram,* his mysterious and majestic power. *Ishvara* means "lord" and *aishvaram* "lordly": Krishna's yoga is something he uses as Ishvara, the Lord of the world. Now he begins to show Arjuna something of the nature of the mystery.

17 Rig, Yajur, and Sama are the principal Vedas, the ancient scriptures that are Hinduism's orthodox authority.

20–21 These verses repeat the idea that heaven itself is an impermanent state. After exhausting the store of their good karma, the blessed souls in heaven must be reborn on earth. Only the liberated soul, the one who has found union with Krishna or *brahmanir-*

vana, escapes the round of rebirth and death as a separate, mortal creature.

CHAPTER TEN

This chapter contains many Sanskrit names, which are briefly identified in the Glossary (see p. 111).

18 *Amrita,* "immortal," comes from *a* "not" and *mrita* "mortal." The Greek word *ambrosia* is cognate and has the same meanings: *amrita* is the ambrosia of the gods, the drink that makes them live forever, and in a general sense it means sweet or nectarlike. So the translation could also be "your words, which are like ambrosia."

22 The mind (*manas*) is here taken to be one of the senses or indriyas of perception; for example, it is really with the mind rather than with the eye that we see.

33 "Among letters I am *A*": perhaps because this is the first letter of the Sanskrit alphabet; perhaps also because it is the most frequent. "Among grammatical compounds": Sanskrit grammar has a number of kinds of compound words; the *dvandva* is a type in which two words are joined with equal rank, rather than one being subordinate to the other.

CHAPTER ELEVEN

14 Here Arjuna presses the palms of his hands together in the gesture called *anjali,* like one of the commonest Western gestures of prayer. This is the usual form of respectful greeting in India, as well as being used in worship and prayer.

15 Brahma, the Creator (not to be confused with Brahman, the attributeless Godhead, which is beyond the Trinity of creation, preservation, and destruction)

sits within a lotus that grows from the navel of Lord
Vishnu.

17 Here Arjuna sees not his friend Krishna but the Lord
incarnate in Krishna: Vishnu, armed with his tradi-
tional weapons, a club (or mace) and a discus. Not
mentioned in this verse are the two benign symbols
he carries in his other two hands, a conch and a lotus.

CHAPTER TWELVE

1 Arjuna is asking which path is superior, that of knowl-
edge (jnana yoga) or that of love (bhakti yoga).

CHAPTER THIRTEEN

5 This is a list of all the twenty-four categories given in
Sankhya philosophy to describe phenomena in the
field of prakriti.

CHAPTER FIFTEEN

1 The ashvattha is the sacred pipal tree, a kind of fig
often grown in temple compounds in India. The idea
of a "world tree" appears in many ancient cultures.
Here the Gita uses the image of the tree as "upside
down," drawing on the fact that the pipal sends out
aerial roots, making "branches above and below." The
image illustrates the phenomenal world, rooted in
Brahman, complete unity, and branching out into the
apparent diversity of life as it is ordinarily perceived.

13 *Rasatmaka soma* is here translated as "life-giving fluid,"
the nourishment of plants. In Hindu mythology it is
the moon, sometimes called Soma, that nourishes
plants, as the source of the life-giving nectar called
Soma. In the Vedas, soma is an intoxicating, invigo-
rating drink distilled from a plant grown high in the

mountains and drunk by participants in a sacred rit-ual. Scholars have tried to discover what the soma plant might have been, but so far no conclusive iden-tification has been made. Soma also appears as an important god in the Vedas.

CHAPTER SEVENTEEN

27–28 *Sat* means that which is real or true and that which is good; it derives from the Sanskrit verb *as,* "to be," and is directly related to our English word *is.* It is noteworthy that this word *sat* links reality and good-ness, reflecting the idea that good is eternal; it is merely covered from time to time by *asat,* evil, which is temporary and in that sense unreal. *Asat* is formed from *sat* by the addition of the prefix *a-,* "without," very much the way English forms words like *amoral.*

CHAPTER EIGHTEEN

1 *Sannyasa* and *tyaga* both mean renunciation, *sannyasa* from the root *as,* "to cast aside," and *tyaga* from *tyaj,* "to give up."

14 "The divine will" is a translation of *daivam,* which comes from the word *deva,* "god." *Daivam* is some-times translated as "fate," but this is inappropriate in the Gita, which is not at all fatalistic. The Gita does, however, allow a place for God's will or Providence in the affairs of humankind—though of course the dominant force is usually karma, not daivam.

34 "Wealth, pleasure, and respectability": *artha, kama,* and *dharma* are three of the four traditional goals of human life. The fourth and highest goal is *moksha,* salvation. The rajasic personality pursues the three worldly goals; moksha is ignored.

41 The Vedas laid down the fourfold division of society into the classes of brahmin, kshatriya, vaishya, and shudra—roughly priests and intellectuals; warriors and rulers; businessmen, farmers, and craftsmen; and workers and servants.

66 *Dharma* is not used here in the usual sense of law or inner nature but in a rarer meaning: a thing's attribute, condition, or conditioning. Usually *dharma* is used in this sense only in the plural, as here: thus dharma is divine law; dharmas are the innumerable beings, things, emotions, and mental states that make up everyday existence as we experience it. Here, following the root meaning (*dhri,* "to support or hold up"), *sarva-dharman* is translated as "all supports," in the sense of external props, conditioned dependencies. Krishna means "cast off your dependency on everything external, Arjuna, and rely on the Self alone."

GUIDE TO SANSKRIT PRONUNCIATION

Consonants.   Consonants are generally pronounced as in English, but there are some differences. Sanskrit has many so-called aspirated consonants, that is, consonants pronounced with a slight *h* sound. For example, the consonant *ph* is pronounced as English *p* followed by an *h,* as in ha*ph*azard; *bh* is as in a*bh*or. The aspirated consonants are *kh, gh, ch, jh, th, dh, ph, bh.*

> *g* as in *g*old
> *h* " " *h*ome
> *j* " " *J*une

The other consonants are approximately as in English.

Vowels.   Simple Sanskrit vowels—*a, i,* and *u*—have two forms, short and long. The long form is marked with a macron—*ā, ī, ū.* Long vowels are pronounced twice as long as the short, as are the double vowels or diphthongs—*e, ai, o,* and *au.* Thus, in the words *nīla* "blue" and *gopa* "cowherd," the first syllable is held twice as long as the second. One unusual vowel, the "vocalic *r,*" is transliterated here as *ri* for the sake of the English reader.

a as in *u*p	*ri* as in w*ri*tten
ā " " f*a*ther	*e* " " th*ey*
i " " g*i*ve	*ai* " " *ai*sle
ī " " s*ee*	*o* " " g*o*
u " " p*u*t	*au* " " c*ow*
ū " " r*u*le	

THE SPELLING OF SANSKRIT WORDS

To simplify the spelling of Sanskrit words we have used a minimum of diacritical marks, retaining only the long mark (ˉ) for the long vowels in this glossary and omitting the other diacritics that are sometimes used in rendering Sanskrit words into English. Some subtleties of Sanskrit pronunciation, such as the difference between retroflex and dental consonants, are therefore lost. The gain in simplicity, however, seems to outweigh this loss.

adharma "Not dharma." Injustice, evil, anything that goes against moral laws.

advaita Having no duality; the supreme Reality, which is the "One without a second." The word *advaita* is especially used in Vedanta philosophy, which stresses the unity of the Self (Ātman) and Brahman.

ahamkāra [*aham* "I"; *kāra* "maker"] Self-will, separateness.

ahimsā [*a* "not"; *himsā* "violence"] Nonviolence, doing no injury, wishing no harm.

ākāsha Space, sky; the most subtle of the five elements.

Ananta The cosmic serpent on which Vishnu reclines in rest.

Arjuna One of the five Pāndava brothers and an important figure in Indian epic and legend. He is Srī Krishna's beloved disciple and friend in the Bhagavad Gītā.

Aryaman "The noble one," a Vedic god revered as an ancestor of mankind.

asat [*a* "not"; *sat* "truth, goodness"] Untruth; anything unreal, untrue, or lacking in goodness.

ashvattha The pipal tree, a kind of fig; it is regarded as holy and often grows in temple compounds.

Ashvatthāma   A great archer and warrior who is Drona's son.

Ātman   "Self"; the innermost soul in every creature, which is divine.

Bhagavad Gītā   [*Bhagavat* "lord"; *gītā* "song"] "The Song of the Lord," a Hindu scripture that contains the instructions of Srī Krishna.

bhakti   Devotion, worship, love.

bhakti yoga   The Way of Love.

Bhīshma   A revered elder of the Kaurava dynasty who allows himself to be killed by Arjuna in the *Mahābhārata* battle.

Brahmā   God as creator, one of the Hindu Trinity; the others are Vishnu, the Preserver, and Shiva, the Destroyer. *Brahmā,* a word with masculine gender, should not be confused with *Brahman,* which has neuter gender. (See *Brahman.*)

brahmachārya   "Conduct leading to God," self-control, purity.

Brahman   The supreme reality underlying all life, the divine ground of existence, the impersonal Godhead.

brahmanirvāna   "Nirvana in Brahman," the final state of spiritual fulfillment: eternal union with Brahman, the ground of all being.

Brahmavidyā   The science of knowing Brahman.

brahmin   [Skt. *brāhmana*] Literally, a person who strives to know Brahman; in traditional Hindu society, a person of the priestly or learned class.

Brihaspati   The guru or priest of the gods.

Buddha   [from *budh* "to wake up"] "The Awakened One," the title given to the sage Siddhārtha Gautama Shākyamuni after he obtained complete illumination. The Buddha lived and taught in North India during the sixth century B.C.E.

buddhi   Understanding, intelligence; the faculty of discrimination; correct view, idea, purpose.

Chitraratha   "Having a bright chariot," the name of the king of Gandharvas.

daivam   Divine will; destiny.

deva   A divine being, a god. The devas of Hindu mythology resemble the Olympians of the ancient Greeks—extraordinary, immortal, yet not unlike mortal men and women in their behavior. The feminine is *devī,* "goddess."

dharma   [from *dhri,* "to support, hold up, or bear"] Law, duty; the universal law that holds all life together in unity.

Dhritarāshtra   The king of the Kurus. He has been blind since birth and has therefore never been enthroned as the rightful king, but he serves as de facto ruler. The entire Bhagavad Gītā is a narration told by Sanjaya to the blind king, whose sons are the Kauravas.

Draupadī   The royal princess who became the wife of each of the five Pāndava brothers.

Drona   A learned brahmin who became a warrior and eventually general of the Kaurava army. The preceptor of the royal princes, he taught the heroes of the *Mahābhārata* the skills of war.

Duryodhana   The oldest son of Dhritarāshtra and the chief enemy of the Pāndavas and Srī Krishna.

gandharva   Heavenly musicians who are demigods, rather touchy and proud, handsome and amorous.

Gāndīva   The name of Arjuna's bow, which was a gift from the god of fire.

Ganges [Skt. *gangā*] A major river of Northern India, looked upon as a sacred symbol.

Garuda The great eagle that is Vishnu's vehicle.

gāyatrī A kind of meter used in the Vedic hymns; a prayer to the sun composed in this meter.

Gītā "The Song," a shorter title for the Bhagavad Gītā.

guna Quality; specifically, the three qualities that make up the phenomenal world: *sattva,* law, harmony, purity, goodness; *rajas,* energy, passion; and *tamas,* inertia, ignorance. The corresponding adjectives are *sattvic, rajasic,* and *tamasic.*

Hastināpura "City of the elephants," an important city in ancient India, about sixty miles northeast of the modern Delhi. It was the capital of the Pāndavas and their line.

Himālaya [*hima* "snow"; *alaya* "abode"] The great mountain range that stretches across the northern border of India, important in mythology as the home of Shiva and other gods.

Ikshvāku The son of Manu and founder of the great Solar Dynasty of kings.

Indra The god of storms and battle. In the Veda, Indra is the chief of the gods (devas) and an important deity; later his role is greatly diminished.

Īshvara The Lord; God.

Janaka A king of ancient times who was both an effective ruler and a holy sage.

jnāna [from *jnā* "to know"] Wisdom; higher knowledge.

jnāna yoga The Way of Wisdom.

kāma Selfish desire, greed; sexual desire, sometimes personified as Kāmadeva.

Kāmadhuk "The cow of wishes," who in legend fulfills all desires.

Kapila   Name of a sage, first teacher of the Sānkhya philosophy.

karma   [from *kri* "to do"] Action; former actions that will lead to certain results in a cause-and-effect relationship.

karma yoga   The Way of Action; the path of selfless service.

Karna   A brave warrior who plays an important role in the larger epic but is only mentioned in passing in the Gītā.

Kauravas   "The sons of Kuru," Duryodhana and his brothers, who are the enemies of the Pāndava brothers.

Kripa   A revered teacher of the royal family who also serves as a warrior.

Krishna   ["black"; or from *krish* "to draw, to attract to oneself"] "The Dark One" or "He who draws us to himself," name of an incarnation of Vishnu. Vishnu, the cosmic force of goodness, comes to earth as Krishna to reestablish dharma, or law. Krishna is the friend and adviser of the Pandāva brothers, especially Arjuna, to whom he reveals the teachings of the Bhagavad Gītā. He is the inner Lord, who personifies spiritual love and lives in the hearts of all beings.

kshatriya   A warrior or prince; a member of the ruling class of traditional Hindu society.

kshetra   A field; a place; a sacred place or temple.

Kubera   God of wealth.

kundalinī   "The serpent power," spiritual or evolutionary energy. In yoga literature, kundalinī is described as a force coiled at the base of the spine. Kundalinī may be aroused through meditation and the practice of yoga; then it rises through the subtle body, awakening the higher centers of consciousness.

Kurukshetra "The field of the Kurus," where the *Mahā-bhārata* battle takes place. It is north of the modern city of Delhi.

Mahābhārata Name of the great Indian epic composed some 2,500 years ago, traditionally attributed to the sage Vyāsa. It relates the conflict between the descendants of Pāndu (the forces of light) and those of Dhritarāshtra (the forces of darkness).

manas The mind; specifically, the faculty that registers and stores sensory impressions.

mantram [or *mantra*] A holy name or phrase; a spiritual formula.

Manu The father of the human race, the Hindu equivalent of Adam or the first man.

Mārgashīrsha The lunar month that falls in November–December.

Marīchi A Vedic demigod. The name means "particle of light."

māyā Illusion; appearance, as contrasted with Reality; the creative power of God.

Meru A mythical mountain said to stand at the center of the world or cosmos. The gods dwell on Meru in beautiful cities, amidst flowering gardens.

moksha Liberation, salvation, illumination.

Nakula One of the junior Pāndava brothers.

Nārada The divine musician and sage who is a devotee of Srī Krishna.

nirvāna [*nir* "out"; *vāna* "to blow"] Complete extinction of self-will and separateness; realization of the unity of all life. (See also Notes, 2:72.)

Om [or *Aum*] The cosmic sound, heard in deep meditation; the Holy Word, taught in the Upanishads, which signifies Brahman, the divine ground of existence.

Pāndavas   "The sons of Pāndu," a collective name for Arjuna and his four brothers, Yudhishthira, Bhīma, Nakula, and Sahadeva. The Pāndavas are in conflict with the Kauravas; both claim the ancient throne of Hastināpura. The Gītā is placed on the eve of the battle that will decide this conflict. The Pāndavas are looked upon as the forces for good and the Kauravas as wicked usurpers, greedy for wealth and power.

Pantanjali   The author of the *Yoga Sūtras,* a classic description of the way to Self-realization through meditation. Patanjali lived around the second century B.C.E., and his method is sometimes referred to as *rāja yoga.*

Pāvaka   "The purifier," a name for the god of fire.

Prahlāda   A demon prince who was greatly devoted to Vishnu.

Prajāpati   "Lord of offspring," the creator of all beings. Indian myth encompasses many creation stories, and sometimes one great Father, or Prajāpati, is mentioned; sometimes there are seven or more fathers or sages who created all living creatures.

prakriti   The basic energy from which the mental and physical worlds take shape; nature.

prāna   Breath; vital force.

Prithā   Arjuna's mother (also called Kuntī). Arjuna is called Pārtha, "son of Prithā."

Purusha   ["person"] The soul; the spiritual core of every person. In the Gītā, the terms *Ātman* and *Purusha* are virtually interchangeable.

rāja yoga   "The Royal Path"; the path of meditation taught especially by Patanjali in the *Yoga Sūtras.*

rajas   See under *guna.*

Rāma   "Prince of Joy," name of the son of Dasharatha,

who was king of Ayodhyā. Rāma was the famous prince who killed the evil demon Rāvana to reclaim his wife Sītā. He is regarded as an incarnation of Vishnu.

Rik The oldest of the four Vedas, which are the most ancient and sacred of the Hindu scriptures.

Rudras A group of gods associated with storm and destruction. Sometimes the Rudras are mentioned as a group; at other times they are thought of as a single god, Rudra. In later Hinduism, Shiva is called Rudra.

Sahadeva One of the junior Pāndava brothers.

Sāma The Veda of songs and chants. One of the four Vedas.

samādhi Mystical union with God; a state of intense concentration in which consciousness is completely unified.

samsāra The world of flux; the round of birth, decay, death, and rebirth.

Sanjaya The sage who divinely perceives the narrative of the Gītā and reports it to the blind king Dhritarāshtra.

Sānkhya One of the six branches of traditional Hindu philosophy. Sānkhya seeks to liberate the individual *Purusha* (spirit) from *prakriti* (mind and matter) through the knowledge of the ultimate separation of these two realities.

sannyāsa Renunciation.

sat [from *as* "to be"] The Real; truth; goodness.

sattva See under *guna*.

Shankara "Giver of peace," a name of Shiva.

Shiva The third Person of the Hindu Trinity, the other two being Brahmā, the Creator, and Vishnu, the Preserver. Shiva destroys, but he also conquers death.

shraddhā   Faith.

shūdra   The fourth Hindu caste; a worker or servant.

Skanda   A god of war, the son of Shiva; general of the divine forces when they go into battle against the demons.

soma   A drink used in Vedic ritual; the drink of the gods.

Srī   [pronounced *shrī*] A title of respect originally meaning "lord" or "holy."

tamas   See under *guna*.

tyāga   Renunciation.

Upanishads   Ancient mystical documents found at the end of each of the four Vedas.

Ushanas   A sage and poet who appears in the Vedas.

varna   Caste or class; specifically, one of the four general classes of traditional Hindu society.

Varuna   God of waters and the ocean; in the Vedas, the moral overseer of the world.

Vāsuki   The king of the serpents; he lives in the underworld and balances the earth on his serpent hood.

Vedas   [from *vid* "to know"] "Knowledge"; the name of the most ancient Sanskrit scriptures, considered to be a direct revelation from God to the mystics of the past.

vidyā   Knowledge, wisdom; a science or branch of study.

vijnāna   Knowledge, judgment, understanding.

Vishnu   Second in the Hindu Trinity; the Preserver who incarnates himself in age after age for the establishment of dharma and for the welfare of all creatures.

Vivasvat   The sun god, the father of Manu, the ancestor of mankind.

Vrishni   Name of an important clan of ancient Northern India. According to legend the Vrishnis all perished at the end of Krishna's life when their city, Dvāraka, sank into the sea.

Vyāsa   The sage revered as the author of the *Mahābhārata* and the Gītā. He was the father of both Dhritarāshtra and Pāndu, and he gave Sanjaya the power of mystic vision so that he could behold the dialogue between Srī Krishna and Arjuna.

yajna   Offering, sacrifice, worship.

Yajur   One of the four Vedas.

yoga   [from *yuj* "to unite"] Union with God, realization of the unity of all life; a path or discipline that leads to such a state of total integration or unity. *Yoga* is also the name of one of the six branches of Hindu philosophy, and as such is paired with *Sānkhya*.

yogī   A person who practices spiritual disciplines.

Yudhishthira   Arjuna's elder brother, who is famous for his adherence to dharma at all times.

yuga   An age or aeon. In Hindu cosmology there are four *yugas,* representing a steady deterioration in the state of the world. The names of the *yugas* are taken from a game of dice. *Krita yuga* is the age of perfection, followed by *tretā yuga.* The incarnation of Srī Krishna is said to mark the end of the third yuga, *dvāpara.* We are living in the fourth and final yuga, *kali,* in which the creation reaches its lowest point. The world goes through one thousand such *yuga* cycles during one *kalpa* or Day of Brahma.

SUGGESTIONS FOR FURTHER READING

EASWARAN, EKNATH. *The Bhagavad Gita for Daily Living.* 3 vols. Berkeley, Calif.: Blue Mountain Center of Meditation, 1975; Tomales, Calif.: Nilgiri Press, 1979, 1984. English translation with extensive practical commentaries on each verse.

————. *The Upanishads.* Tomales, Calif.: Nilgiri Press, 1987. Introduction and English translations of the principal Upanishads and selected others, with introductions to each and a concluding essay by Michael N. Nagler.

————. *Dialogue with Death.* Tomales, Calif.: Nilgiri Press, 1981. A commentary on the Katha Upanishad, providing a practical overview of the main ideas of the Upanishads and Sankhya philosophy.

HUXLEY, ALDOUS. *The Perennial Philosophy.* 1945. Reprint. New York: Harper & Row, 1970.

PRABHAVANANDA, SWAMI. *The Spiritual Heritage of India.* New York: Doubleday, 1963. Reliable, readable history of the sources and schools of religion and philosophy in India.

RADHAKRISHNAN, SARVEPALLI. *The Bhagavadgita.* 1948. Reprint. New York: HarperCollins, 1994. Sanskrit text with English translation and an excellent introduction and notes for those who would like to get close to the original.

EKNATH EASWARAN was director of the Blue Mountain Center of Meditation, which he founded in 1961 in Berkeley, California, after coming to the United States on the Fulbright exchange program as a professor of English literature in 1959. He is the author of many books on the practice of the spiritual life, including *Meditation* (1978), *Gandhi the Man* (1972), and *Take Your Time: Finding Balance in a Hurried World* (1994).

JOHN F. THORNTON is a literary agent, former book editor, and the coeditor, with Katharine Washburn, of *Dumbing Down* (1996) and *Tongues of Angels, Tongues of Men: A Book of Sermons* (1999). He lives in New York City.

SUSAN B. VARENNE is a New York City high school teacher with a strong avocational interest in and wide experience of spiritual literature (M.A., The University of Chicago Divinity School; Ph.D., Columbia University).

EASTERN SPIRITUAL CLASSICS

THE ESSENTIAL GANDHI
An Anthology of His Writings on His Life, Work, and Ideas
by Mahatma Gandhi
Edited by Louis Fischer

"Gandhi believed in revealing himself. He regarded secrecy as the enemy of freedom—not only the freedom of India but the freedom of man. In nearly a half-century of prolific writing, speaking, and subjecting his ideas to the test of actions, he painted a detailed self-portrait of his mind, heart, and soul. And his words have been preserved as they came from his mouth and pen." —Louis Fischer
Autobiography/0-394-71466-0

TAO TE CHING
by Lao Tsu
Translated by Gia-fu Feng and Jane English

The esoteric but infinitely practical *Tao Te Ching,* written in China most probably in the sixth century B.C., has been translated into English more often than any other book except the Bible. This illustrated reissue includes a new introduction and commentary by Jane English, as well as samples of Japanese calligraphy.

"A most useful, as well as beautiful, volume. What it has to say is exactly what the world, in its present state, needs to hear."
—Alan Watts
Religion/Eastern Studies/0-679-77619-2

THE WAY OF ZEN
by Alan Watts

By far the most comprehensive work on Zen that has yet been written by a Westerner, *The Way of Zen* is an explicit and orderly account of Zen Buddhism.

"For either the student or the scholar *The Way of Zen* is an exciting and rewarding experience." —Jean Burden, *Prairie Schooner*
Eastern Philosophy/0-375-70510-4

Available at your local bookstore, or call toll-free to order:
1-800-793-2665 (credit cards only).

VINTAGE SPIRITUAL CLASSICS

THE BOOK OF JOB
Preface by Cynthia Ozick
Religion/Spirituality/0-375-70022-6

CONFESSIONS
by St. Augustine
Translated by Maria Boulding, O.S.B.
Preface by Patricia Hampl
Religion/Spirituality/0-375-70021-8

THE DESERT FATHERS
Translated and Introduced by Helen Waddell
Preface by M. Basil Pennington, O.C.S.O
Religion/Spirituality/0-375-70019-6

THE IMITATION OF CHRIST
by Thomas à Kempis
Edited and Translated by Joseph N. Tylenda, S.J.
Preface by Sally Cunneen
Religion/Spirituality/0-375-70018-8

THE LITTLE FLOWERS OF ST. FRANCIS OF ASSISI
Edited by and Adapted from a Translation by W. Heywood
Preface by Madeleine L'Engle
Religion/Spirituality/0-375-70020-X

THE RULE OF SAINT BENEDICT
Edited by Timothy Fry, O.S.B.
Preface by Thomas Moore
Religion/Spirituality/0-375-70017-X

SELECTED SERMONS, PRAYERS, AND DEVOTIONS
by John Henry Newman
Preface by Peter J. Gomes
Religion/Spirituality/0-375-70551-1

Available at your local bookstore, or call toll-free to order:
1-800-793-2665 (credit cards only).